# ENDORSEMENTS

Cherrie Kaylor's book, *Claiming Your Inheritance*, is an interesting and enlightening encouragement to value what we are hearing from God. Even when we don't realize it is God talking to us, He is talking. The wisdom of writing out your own Scripture book and using it for encouragement, edification, and comfort—i.e., for prophetic purposes—is most helpful. This is a very practical book with practical advice on how to hear God speaking in the whispers of your own spirit and the vital importance of the Bible, the Word of God, in the process. I believe Cherrie's advice will be most helpful to many. An interesting read, not just for the prophets, but for anyone who wants to become more prophetic.

Blessings,
RANDY CLARK, D.MIN.
Founder and President of Global Awakening
and the Apostolic Network of Global Awakening

If a person just follows the Spirit only—they blow up.

If a person just follows the Word only—they dry up.

If a person combines the Word and Spirit—they grow up.

Cherrie Kaylor has written an exciting book, *Claiming Your Inheritance*, which helps the reader to combine Word and Spirit.

The time you spend walking with Cherrie down this sound path will lead you to beautiful life with the Father.

*Claiming Your Inheritance* is a book well worth your time.

Roberts Liardon
Author of international
bestselling series *God's Generals*
Sarasota, Florida

Through the pages of her book *Claiming Your Inheritance*, Cherrie Kaylor uses the Word of God in such an invaluable way. Encouraging us to create our own books, she leads us through a rich process, including handwriting Scriptures and listening to the Father whisper spiritual truths, specifically for each individual. The goal in this journey is not filling up your book but experiencing Him for yourself. I like that we all have different Scripture manuals that are uniquely ours, but we can use them to pray the Word of God for others in need. Cherrie's writings are definitely a beneficial resource to empower this generation to access more of the Kingdom of God.

Heidi G. Baker, Ph.D.
Co-Founder and Director of Iris Global

The apostle James wrote, "We have not, because we ask not." I believe we "ask not" because we fear being disappointed. We fear that maybe the Father won't hear us, won't respond, that maybe He is too much like a human that we looked up to that let us down, thus we hold back our hearts.

Cherrie Kaylor, as a prophetess with a mother's heart of gold, gently draws out your heart and encourages you back into trusting your heavenly Father. The subtitle says it all: we have "unlimited access." We need no longer hold back in fear.

The Father wants to speak to that deep place in each of us, to touch our vulnerable heart and bring transformation. He is completely trustworthy, He is unconditional, and He is perfect love.

Cherrie gives practical tools for growing closer to the Lord and maturing your walk in the Spirit. This book is not simply to be read; it is to be lived. I will make you a promise: if you do the practical steps in this book and draw near to the Lord, He will draw near to you too.

DR. JONATHAN WELTON
Bestselling author and
President of Welton Academy

Cherrie Kaylor's new book, *Claiming Your Inheritance,* can quicken your spirit to become all God created you to be. Used effectively, her Scripture book will be the beginning of true transformation in your life. Your heart's cry for intimacy with God can become a reality. You will be able to hear the voice of God as the Bible comes alive. You will come to realize that you truly do have "unlimited access"!

GARY OATES

Author, *Open My Eyes, Lord,* and

international conference speaker

Cherrie's book is much like Cherrie: beautiful, charming, practical, personable and powerful in the Holy Spirit. It can be easily read by both men and women because the principles are biblical and therefore genderless.

You'll love the conversational style in which Cherrie writes because it includes you, the reader, in her life-long pursuit of God, making you want to pursue God with equal fervency and faithfulness. If you too would like a fruitful, effective life like that of the Kaylors, it would do you well to read this book and emulate its principles.

LARRY TITUS

President, Kingdom Global Ministries

In *Claiming Your Inheritance* Cherrie has done a masterful job of reminding us that the inheritance we leave our children, grandchildren, and future generations goes far beyond material possessions. They need a recorded history of events in our lives and explanation of how through Scripture and prayer, God has directed our family and our business. They deserve the right to the ground we have taken in our lifetime. They need to have documentation of specific battles we have fought and the victories that came because we were partnering with God throughout these challenges. *Claiming Your Inheritance* has inspired me to begin such a book.

RICHARD HOLCOMB
Global Awakening Board Member and
Leadership Team Member
Impact Christian Fellowship
Kerrville, Texas

Before claiming an inheritance, you must know that an inheritance is available and how to claim it. It requires proof that it belongs to you. Inheritance must be defined and transferred before you can benefit by being the owner. Cherrie Kaylor, in her gracious and insightful way, uses deep biblical truths and practical experience to craft a blueprint so you can access all that God has for your life. Enjoy your journey to live in total fulfillment.

DEVI TITUS
Author/speaker and Vice President,
Kingdom Global Ministries

"A strong tool for getting you to the next level."

I read more books than most. Often an issue is better addressed with books in the general mainstream that are not necessarily spiritually based. Then there are books by authors I just automatically buy—books that reach across the spectrum. Cherrie writes to both ends of the rainbow. Those are my favorite books.

Like all she has published, this is an encouraging and practical book to add to your toolkit. Cherrie has given you and me a gift. Pick it up. Read it. Read it again. Walk it! No matter your location, your life will change. (Pardon, I almost forgot—first pay for it!)

STEVE SJOGREN
Kindness.com

It was the obligation of the king of Israel to write the law of God in his own handwriting in the presence of the priest so that he would know and do the Word of God. Cherrie teaches us, as kings and priests, the tremendous value, in every circumstance of life, in writing His special revealed promises that are whispered to us and having them come alive and take root in our hearts and lives. A royal, priestly fruit is seen in Cherrie's life and ministry. I urge you to listen and follow her as she follows her Lord. You also will be transformed and blessed as a king and priest of God.

ROBERT BARRON
Attorney and teacher

# Claiming
## YOUR
# Inheritance

# Claiming YOUR Inheritance

UNLIMITED ACCESS TO THE
*Voice of God*

Cherrie Kaylor

DESTINY IMAGE® PUBLISHERS, INC.
P.O. Box 310, Shippensburg, PA 17257-0310
*"Promoting Inspired Lives."*

This book and all other Destiny Image and Destiny Image Fiction books are available at Christian bookstores and distributors worldwide.

Cover design by: Eileen Rockwell

For more information on foreign distributors, call 717-532-3040.
Reach us on the Internet: www.destinyimage.com.

ISBN 13 TP: 978-0-7684-0798-3
ISBN 13 eBook: 978-0-7684-0799-0

For Worldwide Distribution, Printed in the U.S.A.
1 2 3 4 5 6 7 8 / 19 18 17 16 15

# DEDICATION

I dedicate this book to the love of my life, my dearest friend, my husband Michael. You are a man after God's heart, filled with truth, peace, integrity, and honor. You are my balance. Your life has given me wings to fly. You have provided a home in which it is safe to learn and discover the things of God, filling it with music and God's presence. You have covered me, healed me, grown my heart and mind, and it is to you I give my life and love forever.

I also dedicate this book to our amazing children. To our daughter Stephanie… you have become a great woman of God with wisdom beyond your years. Your compassion and merciful heart are changing the lives of everyone who knows you. Your steadfast faith in God is an example even to me. Your strength and sacrifice and determination not to settle for anything less than God's purposes are a treasure, and seen in the beauty of your first love—your heart toward God.

To our daughter Tiffany… your heart has been filled with the song of the Lord all your life. You have pressed the presence of God and pulled music from God's own heart, giving it to us that we may see the Father afresh. You have filled our mouths and hearts with worship and words to express our love to Him. You have an unwavering heart for the Father and possess wisdom beyond your years.

To our son Michael David...you are a man of God, whose joyful heart since birth has lifted me more than you will ever realize. Your heart for the lost is so amazing. You risk more than most to reach them and help them to understand their value in the Father's eyes. You are our son in whom I am well pleased.

To Lucas, our precious son-in-law...you are an integral part of who we are as a family and help complete our family. You add such fresh value to us all.

To Tiffany and Lucas's children Isabella Grace, Liam Alexander, and Guinevere Ann...you have opened to me a whole new realm of God and His amazing love. Your lives reveal dimensions of the Father I have never experienced before. Your love has changed my world.

A special thanks to Robert Barron, a man of God who makes the Word of God delicious every time he teaches. Your encouragement made this book happen. You and Laurie are treasured friends who have been an integral part of what ministry is in our life.

This project is available today because of an excellent craftsman and woman of God, Susan Thompson. You polished my rough edges and allowed this to shine with the brightest light available. Thank you for your many hours and expertise.

To our friend Randy Clark, who has put feet to the love of God in sending us to the nations and who believed in us as we lived this tool in the nations.

To my family, friends, and members of our church who have created and used their Scripture books and are now seeing how it makes a difference in the destiny of others—how these living books help to advance the Kingdom of God to change the course of the future and bring us face to face with the Father. It is a joy to watch the Word transform lives.

To you, the reader...I give to you from the treasure of my life and from my spiritual inheritance so that your inheritance and that which you pass to your future generations may be enriched. I spiritually impart to you through these pages what God has placed in me—that which I have fought for, bled for, and have learned—so that you might have a fuller measure of His glory in you, pressed down, shaken together, and running over.

# CONTENTS

Preface. . . . . . . . . . . . . . . . . . . . . . . . . . . . . 17

Introduction . . . . . . . . . . . . . . . . . . . . . . . 23

CHAPTER 1  Developing a Spiritual Sensitivity
to God's Voice. . . . . . . . . . . . . . . . . . . . . 35

CHAPTER 2  How to Begin Your Scripture Book. . . . . 45

CHAPTER 3  The Transformation is in
Using the Book . . . . . . . . . . . . . . . . . . . . 59

CHAPTER 4  As a Weapon of Intercession . . . . . . . . . . 73

CHAPTER 5  Building Your Faith . . . . . . . . . . . . . . . . 87

CHAPTER 6  Prophetic Direction. . . . . . . . . . . . . . . . 105

CHAPTER 7  A Counseling Tool . . . . . . . . . . . . . . . . .117

CHAPTER 8  A Sermon and Teaching Tool . . . . . . . . 127

CHAPTER 9  Journaling the Visions, Dreams,
and Revelations. . . . . . . . . . . . . . . . . . . . 133

AFTERWORD  How Do I Start My Scripture Book?. . . 139

APPENDIX  How Can I Know Jesus? . . . . . . . . . . . . 143

# PREFACE

One evening, the pure pursuit of intimacy compelled our daughter to sit alone in the recording studio with the lights dimmed. After the sound engineers had gone home, she poured her heart out to the Lord in worship. As she began to play, she pulled out of her spirit a song of intimacy expressed to the Father, with the lyrics "I want to be closer to You." I believe this is the heart cry of every pilgrim who desires a richer life with God and an understanding of the essence of what it means to walk with Him. Anyone who is truly on this journey can never be content with only knowing about God. We must personally know God and be completely and utterly known by Him.

At one point my husband Michael and I were seeking, fasting, and praying for direction as to how we could better equip the Body of Christ. There was a deep yearning for growth for the whole Church, and for the local church as well. As we sought God, He illuminated the idea of making Scripture books as a tool for the advancement of the Kingdom in the personal walk of the believer. At one point I heard Him say, "One voice, the voice of My Word, should be on the lips of My Bride. No matter who a seeker speaks to, My Word on their lips will reach the lost and heal a dying world."

We, as a Church, must remember the great value of God's written Word as the source that reveals His character. The Bible tells us, "There is nothing new under the sun," and yet we find ourselves in a time of increased revelation and empowerment for the Body of Christ (Ecclesiastes 1:9). We are encouraged by Old Testament prophets to seek knowledge and understanding. In Psalms and Proverbs, we are repeatedly told to obtain and hold on to understanding and wisdom.

We are encouraged to meditate on the Scriptures day and night (see Josh. 1:8; Ps. 1:2), to be washed with the water of the Word (see Eph. 5:26), to renew our minds with the Word of God (see Rom. 12:1-2), and to think on these things, whatsoever is pure and just (see Phil. 4:8).

There is such a battle for our attention in the world today. The enemy tries to distract us from advancing the Kingdom in our personal life and through the Church by breaking down the local church and the global Church. In the midst of all this, the idea of pursuing God in a place of intimacy and freedom can seem out of reach to the average believer in Jesus.

While we often think of the great desires of our heart to do mighty deeds that will lead many to the Lord, we can forget that the first "kingdom" to be taken by the Word of God is the kingdom of our own heart. I believe that as forerunners come forth and demonstrate what the normal Christian life is really meant to look like, it will become evident that the Church at large has fallen short of the high calling of God in Christ Jesus. I propose that we start strengthening ourselves by feasting on the revelation found in the Bible. God is faithful to fill our hunger with His Word as we seek Him.

The Lord told a depressed Elijah that there were seven thousand who were loyal to Him, even though their identities were unknown to Elijah himself (see 1 Kings 19:9-21). God is the Lord who lives and sees. He sees the hungry heart yearning for Him. Our King sees all who are hungry for more of the Kingdom, all who are pressing into the high calling while teaching and leading others to do the same. I believe that this holy hunger will be satisfied. The whisper of one hungry heart will not go unheard over the legions of voices in the earth today.

I became an active minister at the age of seventeen and have seen signs and wonders all my life. My heritage is rich with great men and women of God. One of the greatest joys in ministry for me is watching the rapid growth of a believer in his or her walk with God, no matter the stage of his or her journey.

I have worked for Fortune 500 companies, advancing through the ranks by the grace of God. He has given me the gift of understanding the needs of a company and the wisdom to apply what is beneficial My education was not the key, but God's Word always was. "I can do all things though [Christ] who strengthens me" (Philippians 4:13). This is a life lesson my father lived out in front of me and gave as an inheritance by example, and it became part of my life as well.

During these years in the corporate world, as I traveled, I would use every opportunity to share the gospel. I noticed without question how often people would avoid me if I was reading my Bible.

Over time I noticed that when I had my Scripture book with me, people were much more open to receive. When talking to someone on a plane, I would simply say, "I wrote down a Scripture the other day that might help your situation." Then I would turn to my notebook to get a Scripture, and ninety percent of the time they would read it with me. Then I would write down the Scripture so that they could take it with them. It was like drawing flies to sugar. Their defenses were down since I was not a preacher trying to convert them. I was simply a knowledgeable person who had an answer for their heart.

The idea of a Scripture book is simple yet profound. As we explore life with God, we can record our journey for others so that they can inherit the wisdom of our experiences. It is my desire to share with you how you can create your own Scripture book thatyou too can use to leave an inheritance for your children and grandchildren so that they may have the privilege of running where you now walk and flying where you now run. Join with me and discover some very practical ways to live and preach God's Word, to encourage both the believer and the unbeliever. Journey with me to the impossible that only God makes possible.

# INTRODUCTION

I believe that the longing for God that we feel in our hearts has always been there and will always be there because we are flooded with the DNA of the Father, the Divine Creator of all things who is Himself eternal. We feel the pulling and the yearning toward the eternal things of God, and that longing will not end until we see Him face to face. Yet at some point in our journey, we become aware that our destiny is not random but has purpose that comes from God. It is at this point that we can shift from random journeying to a purposeful journey, if we choose.

For years my journey seemed to be about growth and education, and I know many are still on that path. But as I grew in discernment, there came a Holy Spirit whisper that called from God's Kingdom. It was a whisper that brought clarity where none existed before. This whisper comes as a voice that is heard but is not always understood. It forges a path that takes me out of the realm of the natural into God's presence. It is a place where abundance, peace, and love overflow.

When I am in the midst of the overflow of these fruits, I am highly aware of the blessings of being on such a path. I can sense the yearning in my heart to walk this path, to take freely of the abundance, and to give it away to those who don't yet see or hear but only hunger and thirst.

From this path I can clearly see the radiant vistas of peace, abundance, joy, intimacy, confidence, under-standing, wisdom, and above all love. I believe we all yearn for these vistas, but yearning alone will not get us there. We must choose to seek God's invitation, then accept it and walk in it.

If you have always felt that there must be more, then you are aware of what I am saying. If you have seen people whose lives overflow with an abundance of the fruits of the Spirit, you are most likely seeing those who walk this path of radiant vistas. The chapters to follow are an invitation to you, a field guide, to a life spent walking upon the heights of intimacy with the Lord Jesus and with our magnificent heavenly Father and the Holy Spirit. If and when you make the choice to take this journey, your walk will shift from random-ness to awareness. Actually, this choice is more than a journey; it is a pilgrimage, a holy quest, and there will be times when it will not be easy. You may sacri-fice much, but know that the value of your sacrifice is what God will receive. You alone determine the value of what you do and what you give.

As with any expedition, especially one to uncharted realms and territories, you'll need the right gear. The first thing in your pack should be the full armor of God (see Eph. 6:10-17). Put it on every day without fail, and let this be your first clue that it is a battle you are going into, not a picnic.

I once read a fantasy saga about a young warrior on a quest who carried his mother's sword, forged by her own hands. He could feel the power of her life in the sword. Mother and son spoke of the forging of the sword as a holy thing, a connection to something deeper of God, something that revealed His perfection. I want to teach you about this holy thing, this deep place of God—about the art of creating a living sword that you can use on a daily basis. This holy thing, this sword, is the living Word of God residing in you.

To forge such a sword will take time and purpose; it won't happen overnight. You will need to reach into the realms of heaven and pull down those living elements that will forge this two-edged sword within you. But once it is formed, you will find yourself able to destroy the works of the enemy and bring healing to those who have been wounded by the evil one. The mouth of God Himself, and His Son, will enable you to do this in the power of the Holy Spirit.

Along your journey transformation is inevitable. You will become the living Word of God, and the higher inner path will be where you walk. The King-dom of God will become yours.

This is the inheritance you can give to your gen-erations to come and to others. They will feel what is on your sword, in your life, and in your journey. The whole world dreams of such an inheritance; countless stories have been written about it and movies made, but it is Jesus—and He alone—who can offer you this journey and this life, if you accept His invitation. What has opened your eyes—the experience of time and education or the Word of God and His Spirit?

Listen to what the apostle John writes of Jesus:

> *In the beginning was the Word, and the Word was with God, and the Word was God* (John 1:1).

> *And the Word became flesh, and dwelt among us, and we saw His glory, glory as of the only begot-ten from the Father, full of grace and truth* (John 1:14).

Jesus came and dwelt among us. His finished work on the cross is the gateway for the Body of Christ. The shift in our lives can begin at this gateway if we choose to put our feet upon His new path.

When we make the choice to step through the nar-row gate, we will find ourselves on *the* path of destiny and purpose with Jesus Christ, the true source of truth and life who is the power of the living Word. He will become our Facilitator. No longer will we be tossed about by every wind of chance, separated from God.

We will display the glory of God, just as everything created is a display of His glory.

I believe that one of our purposes as believers is to become the living Word of God. We were created to walk in the full inherent authority given to us at the cross. It is from this place of authority that we destroy the works of the enemy. A life lived in the fullness of Christ takes more than memorizing a few Scriptures, more than praying the Word of God over our lives and those for whom we intercede. We must be transformed into the living image of Christ by the power of the living Word.

Only the transformed life can become a living Word in season, through unwavering relationship with the Father. Do you live by every Word that proceeds from the mouth of God? Daily conversations with God keep the Scriptures both true and "in season" in our hearts. The Word of God must be a "present" Word for us—it must be a "now" Word.

Have you ever memorized a Bible verse only to find yourself limited by that memorized verse when you move into a new season of your life? Memorization alone is not enough. There must be revelation that accompanies the Word if it is to come alive in our hearts. This "life" is the whisper of the Spirit of God on the Word, and it is in this life that we find insight into the Father's heart. It is this life that pulls dimensions of healing and the power of freedom and love from the living Word.

If we quote the Word of God but do not live it, we have form without power, religion but not relationship. Much of the Body of Christ today is caught in the snare of religion. We must be daring enough to take the sword of the Spirit and cut through the dull cobwebs of compliancy, lethargy, and convenient programs, and move boldly into a holy quest for freedom and revelation, where we will meet God face to face as a companion and a friend.

We need the transformation of the Word of God in our lives if we are to be changed from lesser glory to greater glory. We are all "being transformed into the same image from glory to glory" by the Spirit of the Lord as we press into an intimate walk with God (2 Corinthians 3:18).

As the living Word of God transforms us, we will find our selves in a constant state of growing and maturing, where the Word is not just an idea or a thought but a living, spiritual substance that is growing in us and causing growth in us. Jesus said that His words are Spirit and Life with the power to heal and make us whole (see John 6:63). It is His living Word that unveils the spotless Bride (the Church) for whom Jesus is returning.

The living Word of God is not limited to a particular time or a specific dimension. Rather, as our relationship with the Father grows in depth and understanding, so will the Word of God grow in us and create new life in us and through us. This intimate relationship with God is a worthy and obtainable goal. It is a hedge and a sword, water in the wilderness. It brings life to the things of God and death to the schemes of the enemy. Every nuance of it is important.

The living Word of God will orchestrate the fullness of life in us. Think of it—the fullness of life! We have been created for a purpose, and each one of us has a destiny. This is the cry of the heart.

To be a disciple literally means to be a "learned one." We study the Word to show ourselves to be approved unto our God (see 2 Tim. 2:15). And we study to renew our minds in order for the reality of the Kingdom of God to come into our lives, as He interacts with us moment by moment. This interaction is His constant revelation to our minds, giving us spiritual comprehension of His glory. It was the cry of Moses when he prayed, "Show me Your glory!" and the heart cry of Paul when he wrote to the Philippians, "That I may know Him" (Exodus 33:18; Philippians 3:10).

This "life" will be revealed by what we leave as an inheritance for future generations. Although we study and discipline ourselves in order to remove all barriers of distraction and confusion that limit us from the fullest experience of our completely limitless God, study in and of itself is not the passion of this quest. Study is one of the mountains we travel and climb, but it is in the journey that study unveils the vistas of glory and insight, and ultimately companionship with the Father.

I use the discipline of study, but only as a tool to open the gate between time and eternity. I have discovered that I am an eternal being already, walking through time with my limited experience, while possessing the tools God created for me to use in the battle to attain victory in my life. George Otis, Jr., puts it this way: "We see a tiny fragment of reality, which allows us to master our physical environment and very little more."[1] I think he is referring to our consciousness. How often do we confuse reality with what we need rather than what truly exists? When we live with the consciousness of a God who knows no impossibility, we will find the courage to live radically. We will never fall short of dreaming the biggest dreams or lose the ability to grow from glory to glory (see 2 Cor. 3:18).

The Holy Spirit alone illuminates our mind and spirit to greater depths of knowledge, experience, and wisdom. John Wimber taught that supernatural living is the normal Christian lifestyle.[2] Every believer can move in the miraculous by the power of the Holy Spirit. If we settle for non-miraculous Christianity, we will find our minds caught in a battle between true Christianity and religion.

Our intuitive responses to supernatural stimuli have been desensitized. As a result, we often must battle old habits and dulled thinking when we try to tap into the eternal part of our being, our spirit. While many believers are able to discover clues to this kind of supernatural living through consistent pure-hearted inquiry, these clues become valuable only when they are enriched, revealed, and interpreted by the Holy Spirit. It is at this point that our spirits can begin the journey of comprehension.

This tool you are about to forge, this journey you are about to take, is for empowering—the empowering of your comprehension. But you must not just hold this tool in your hand. You must wield it. You must do something with it.

God did not pour out His power for us to sit each Sunday in our "good people clubs" and pat each other's spiritual egos. The power from heaven was and is given to make us dangerous: dangerous to the god of this world, as we employ God's power to destroy the enemy's works; dangerous because the truth has set us free from the bonds of the fall of Adam and free from the dominating enemy. This kind of freedom will keep us living on the edge, where sin has lost its power and where death has no sting (see 1 Cor. 15:54-55).

Radical obedience comes from an awareness of a God who has no limitations. O what joy to wake up each morning bathed in His presence and exercised by the Spirit, as He equips us afresh for our divine assignment to change the destiny of the world in which we live. Jesus called the twelve to be with Him (see Mark 3:14-19). God is looking for those who seek and hunger after His face, those who want to know Him and who dare to be with Him.

When we devote ourselves to God, we become more than who we are presently. When we study the Word of God, we become pregnant with His revelation. Being devoted is being connected, and the two become one by the power of His Word.

Peter speaks of the living Word of God as the "seed" (see 1 Pet. 1:23). In Greek, *seed* means "sperma," that by which we have been born again. The Word as sperma is a picture of the marriage bed in which the heavenly Father and the Bride meet, conceiving the mysteries of heaven. With this meeting there is a pregnancy that takes place—that is, the revelation of His Son within us that God has fathered. As God's living Word comes into our lives, we open our spirit and understanding to receive revelation and experiential knowledge.

God is always faithful to nurture the revelations He places in our life. Every revelation is a seed that has the ability to become the imprint of truth and revelation within us. And God our Father will supply that seed of revelation and everything necessary to bring forth a full harvest *if* we will be diligent to seek His face.

In the pages of this book, I will show you how to create a tool—your own Scripture book—that will help you deepen devotion, facilitate conception, and bring God's revelation to full maturity within you so that you may be better equipped to fight the battle and walk in the harvest of God's Kingdom. Understand that the spiritual battle always takes place in the mind. Your Scripture book will become your field guide to intimacy and friendship with your heavenly Father so that your mind can become conformed to the mind of Christ (see Rom. 12:2). Your consciousness will expand to include the impossible, and your passion and power will be exercised. You will develop purpose for the divine in your life.

We all need a purpose-driven life. When the reality that Jesus is more than enough and that nothing is impossible with God takes root and comes to fruition in your life, you will become dangerously confident in all that can "be" with God.

The Spirit and the Bride (the Church) long for you to discover the absolute resolve of God living in you, which is the reality of His Kingdom right here, right now. And "the Spirit and the bride say, 'Come'" (Revelation 22:17). I believe that to be the spotless Bride *now* means to walk in the full authority of His grace for the Body of Christ in these days. It is an obtainable goal. His Word says He is coming back for His spotless Bride.

We must contend for our generation to herald the Good News that His Word is true and that we can walk in the fullness of it. When we do this, we will see generations become overcomers who walk in divine health and intimacy with the Father.

> *"And I saw the dead, great and small, standing before the throne, and books were opened. Another book was opened, which is the book of life..."* (Revelation 20:12 NIV).

## NOTES

1.  George Otis, Jr., *The Twilight Labyrinth* (Bloomington, IN: Chosen Books, 1997), 64.

2.  John Wimber, *Power Evangelism* (Ventura, CA: Regal Books, 1986, 2009).

## Chapter 1

# DEVELOPING A SPIRITUAL SENSITIVITY TO GOD'S VOICE

*Now may the God of peace Himself sanctify you
entirely; and may your spirit and soul and body be
preserved complete, without blame at the coming
of our Lord Jesus Christ. Faithful is He who
calls you, and He also will bring it to pass.*

—1 THESSALONIANS 5:23-24

## QUANTUM THEORY APPLIED TO OUR LIFE

You are about to develop a tool for your life, for your ministry, and for intimacy with the Father. As you begin this journey of creating a Scripture book, let's consider for a moment a few facts that may broaden your experience.

As believers, we should understand that we are a spirit, we have a soul, and we live in a physical body. Our spirit being is eternal. Our soul consists of our mind, our will, and our emotions, which create conscious thoughts. We have a physical body in which we dwell. Our spirit man operates in the supernatural or the invisible things of life; and though invisible, the supernatural realm has a tangible reality that can be experienced in the natural realm.

Let's apply a bit of quantum theory to this understanding. Quantum theory teaches us that the average human is receiving four hundred billion bits of information through our five senses every second. We filter all this information down to about two hundred thousand bits that we call "consciousness." That consciousness includes height, width, depth, and time, which we identify as the four dimensions we live in and observe moment by moment.

My logical speculation or theory is that our spirit was designed and is capable of greater perception, and that the Spirit-led life perceives and processes more than two hundred thousand bits of information per second. Think of it for a moment—our spirit is receiving this vast information "download" every second. Stated another way, in this computer age, there is no "bandwidth limitation" in the realm of the spirit. However, whether because of experience or lack of experiential understanding, we are not cognitively assimilating all the billions of bits of stimuli that are available to our spirit every second of every day.

Look for a moment at the following painting of a galaxy and then the next painting of microscopic enhancement. There are many different aspects of the paintings such as the colors and facets of the shapes and the angles. Let your gaze linger on the paintings, and try to process all that you see in them.

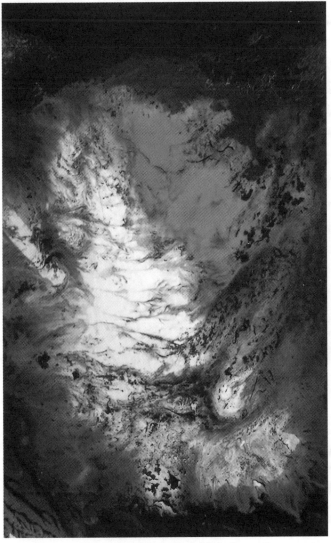

Color images available on KaylorMinistries.com

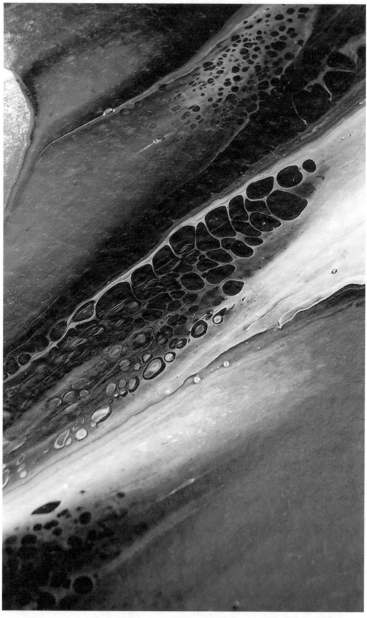

Color images available on KaylorMinistries.com

Contained within these two paintings—from the vastness of space to the minute detail of the microscopic—are all the parameters of two thousand bits of information.

We know that one of the primary functions of the mind is to filter appropriate mental inventory from all the daily stimuli that bombard us so that we may function in the natural world without sensory overload and confusion. However, the redemption of our spirit man and the infilling of the Holy Spirit increases our capacity for spiritual perception.

I think that while our "filtering" may remain the same, our awareness of the divine interaction with our senses will heighten, expanding our comprehension of the world around us. As this happens, we can begin to understand and perceive that which was previously invisible. Christ tells us the Kingdom of God is here now. But how do we tune into it? How are we to connect with it?

Could it be that the Kingdom of God is being communicated to us in the four hundred billion bits of information that we receive daily and we have been blind and deaf to it? We all need the touch of God, and we all need the breath of God to blow upon us. This will open us up so that we may comprehend the reality of His voice, which is constantly speaking. The Scriptures tell us that God said:

> "Go and tell this people: 'Keep on listening, but do not perceive: Keep on looking, but do not

*understand.' "Render the hearts of this people insensitive, their ears dull, and their eyes dim, otherwise they see with their eyes, hear with their ears, understand with their hearts, and return and be healed"* (Isaiah 6:9-10).

God is waiting to open the ears and eyes of those who diligently seek Him so that we may comprehend our inheritance, which is given to us to be used as a weapon against the enemy.

Now consider for a moment how much more you have filtered your life, omitting understanding and knowledge in order to focus on your day-to-day routine. And then consider how much you allow that simple routine to determine what you do with this magnificent creation called "you." You filter the two hundred thousand bits of information down to a few thousand by subconscious routine and call that severely limited awareness your "life."

## WHAT GOD IS DOING WITH "LIFE?"

Let us now consider what the Spirit of the Lord is doing with what God calls "life." In the living Word and the baptism of the Holy Spirit and the renewing of our minds, He is, through the Spirit of prophecy, giving understanding and causing our true humanity in Christ to arise. He wants each one of us to understand who He is calling us to be. On top of this, He is also revealing to us the greatness that is within us. He wants to call this greatness forth through a new awareness and comprehension of the unseen reality of His Kingdom. The Scripture says that by understanding the love of God, we are filled with all the fullness of God. Paul prayed for the Ephesians:

> *So that Christ may dwell in your hearts through faith; and that you, being rooted and grounded in love, may be able to comprehend with all the saints what is the breadth and length and height and depth, and to know the love of Christ which surpasses knowledge, that you may be filled up to all the fullness of God. Now to Him who is able to do far more abundantly beyond all that we ask or think, according to the power that works within us, to Him be the glory in the church* [Bride/ Body of Christ] *and in Christ Jesus to all generations forever and ever. Amen* (Ephesians 3:17-21).

I invite you to increase your awareness and spiritual sensitivity, allowing the Holy Spirit to transform you from one degree of glory to another as you begin to learn the task of focusing on the Master.

As you read this book, radio programs, television shows, movies, cell phone conversations, and smartphone emails are all floating within and through your room in the invisible realm in frequency form. All these frequencies are unseen and silent to you, unless you have a receiver that is able to detect the waves and translate them into recognizable sounds and images.

Turn on the television and change the channel and suddenly the silent, empty room will be filled with images and sounds sent to you from another location, all because you have the proper receiver.

It is the same with heaven's reality—it is in the air all around you right now. When your ears are opened to God and His conversations, the only thing you must do is tune your "receivers" and "translators" to those "waves" in order to perceive His voice to you.

God has so much more for all of us to live in and to walk out. His promise of abundant life is not limited in any way, shape, or form. Only God can give full illumination to our spirit, soul, and mind. However, it is up to us to determine where the strength of our spirit and life will be invested. It is up to us to determine what we will think upon, what we will open our heart to, and what we will keep our mind focused on in the Kingdom of God.

## CAPTURED BY THE SMALLNESS OF OUR MINDS?

We cannot comprehend all that God desires to pour into our hungry hearts. He longs for our mind be renewed in order that we may discover the fullness of the wisdom and understanding that He has for us. We are captured by the smallness of our own mind and our even smaller experiences. We are held prisoner by the very temptation of the Garden of

Eden: "Eat and you will become wise" was the lying promise of the serpent (see Gen. 3:5-6).

You and I were created with this wonderful computer-like mind, hungry for the intake of information. Our mind is like a sponge. But one glaring disappointment in all this is humankind's failure to find wisdom in our pursuit of information. The fall seems to have caused us to fill the space in our spirit that was reserved for wisdom with counterfeit, self-absorbed, self-sufficient control and superiority rather than true wisdom from above. Knowledge can never replace wisdom.

Danny Silk explains this concept with great insight this way:

> The thought that God was withholding the knowledge of good and evil is not valid. I believe that as "the wisdom giver," God intended His children to be learned about evil but only after a healthy and practiced dependence on Him in order to balance the understanding. So the premature download of information caused a hunger in man for immediate gratification and selfishness. They ran from God and made their own covering. The "do it myself" need, motivated by guilt and shame. Oh, how we would rather they had run to the Father and declared their nakedness. But here we all sit in our clothes.[1]

With all these things in mind, it is time to begin the journey of writing your Scripture book. Born out of your relationship with God, your Scripture book will become a journal of your understanding and wisdom from Him. It will be a treasure of revelation from the Father, and an inheritance to your children and your children's children.

I pray that your Scripture book will become an intimate tool that you will use to forge the living sword of God within you, and to discover Him in new and powerful ways. I pray that we would know how to

...ascend Your holy mountain

We will stand in Your presence

And speak to the winds.[2]

I invite you now to discover the forging process of creating your Scripture book. There's no telling where God will lead you!

## NOTES

1. Danny Silk, "What Is Your Name," Bethel (Redding, CA, 2011), http://www.ibethel.org/store/p89/WhatisYourName/product_info.html?browse_authors_id=6.

2. Brian Johnson, "We Believe" © 2004.

## Chapter 2

# HOW TO BEGIN YOUR SCRIPTURE BOOK

*But as for you, Bethlehem Ephrathah, too little to*
*be among the clans of Judah, from you One will go*
*forth for Me to be ruler in Israel. His goings forth*
*are from long ago, from the days of eternity.*
—MICAH 5:2

*Now it shall come about when he sits on the throne of his*
*kingdom, he shall write for himself a copy of this law on*
*a scroll in the presence of the Levitical priests. It shall*
*be with him and he shall read it all the days of his life,*
*that he may learn to fear the Lord his God, by carefully*
*observing all the words of this law and these statutes...*
—DEUTERONOMY 17:18-20

*For who has despised the day of small things?*
—ZECHARIAH 4:10

## PURPOSE OF THE SCRIPTURE BOOK

The purpose of creating a Scripture book is not just about writing down Scriptures that speak to your heart. That in and of itself will have a degree of benefit to your spirit and soul since the Word will not go forth without accomplishing what it was sent to do (see Isa. 55:10-12). However, your Scripture book will be more than that. It will have the unique fingerprint of God for your life and ministry.

If we were to hike the Appalachian Trail together, each one of us would have a slightly different experience, unique to us. I most likely would notice different vistas and different details than you.

God shows us in nature that no two things are alike—not even snowflakes. How many trillions of billions of snowflakes have fallen in your lifetime, and yet the infinite resources of God will not repeat even one, although the structures of almost all will never even be seen by man? Each snowflake is perfect beauty unto itself and will never be fully discovered by a human. But it will be fulfilled in itself as His creation to be an extension of His mind and an expression of His infinite love, which is a perfect expression of His glory.

Though I use some of the same Scriptures in every Scripture book I create, they oftentimes will be used in different categories and with different illumination. Scriptures are not just categorized for the sole discipline of creating categories. Anyone can go to a concordance in order to categorize different portions of Scripture, but the true purpose of the Scripture book lies much deeper than this. Creating your Scripture book will be an experience with God, not simply an exercise of discipline. It may have a small beginning; but much like the little town of Bethlehem, the Ancient of Days reveals Himself from small places.

## DISCOVERING SCRIPTURES TO USE

The only Scriptures that should be put into your book are the ones that have life in them for you—Scriptures that have been illuminated with insight or personal revelation, whispered from the Spirit of God to you intimately These should be Scriptures that have already begun to transform you.

Let me explain what I mean by this. Jesus spoke in parables to thousands of people. The learned and the unlearned were present while He spoke, but His Word, or the truth of the Word, was revealed to the humble and the hungry. The prideful did not understand what He was talking about. Such are the mysteries of God. I once heard Bill Johnson say, "Because there is power in truth He has hidden it from everyone who is not hungry or humble of heart."[1]

Let us remember these words from Matthew 11:

> *At that time Jesus said, "I praise you, Father, Lord of heaven and earth, because you have hidden these things from the wise and learned, and revealed them to little children"* (Matthew 11:25 NIV).

The great I AM is the One who conceals a matter for you to seek out. Proverbs says, "It is the glory of

God to conceal a matter, but the glory of kings is to search out a matter" (Proverbs 25:2). God hides things not *from* us, but *for* us. He doesn't hide things in order for us to never find them; but He hides things in such a way that we will pursue and be able to attain what we seek. I believe God has a mystery that He will hold in heaven for you alone to discover. And if you do not pull it from the depths of His glory by your passion, it will not be revealed.

## THE CREATION OF YOUR SWORD

Any person can create a Scripture book through disciplined effort and have nothing but a bunch of Scriptures put into different categories. I am proposing you do more than that. I am proposing that you craft a tool worthy of the hand of a warrior in the Kingdom of God. Allow God to place His sword in you and sharpen it. Just as the making of a real sword is an intense and laborious process, so is the forging of God's Word within you, but when it is done it can be used for battle with great effectiveness.

To make a sword you must first dig the ore, placing it in the fire until the dross is lifted from it. When the dross has burned away, the ore goes back in the refiner's fire for the process to begin again. When that process is complete, the metal is pounded, reheated, and cooled as the blade is formed and sharpened. In this way, iron sharpens iron until the perfect balance of blade and hilt is achieved. Finally, there is more sharpening and honing of the blade, followed by the final décor and then the seal of the craftsman.

Anyone can buy a plastic sword and pretend to be a warrior, or order a sword through a catalog and add it to their collection. Or, you can pay the price and have one crafted just for you. The most expensive blades in the world are one of a kind. Take, for example, the samurai sword, a sword in which every detail, every step is finishedwith complete accuracy, skipping nothing. It is a sword created for one purpose—to destroy. It can take anywhere from a month to as long as three months to create a single sword of this nature. Likewise, it will take a lot of work to craft God's Word into a sword suited for you alone. Just as a samurai sword will have value for generations to come, so the long-process of allowing God to craft His living Word in you will define the value of it for future generations. When we invest our time to create a Scripture book, what we have will increase in value as an inheritance for our children and our future generations to come.

But most importantly, the sword we create is to be used in our daily lives, to minister to our own souls as well as those whom the Lord sends to us. It is in the creative process that we become the sword. The Word of God is internalized, becoming a part of who we are. Bill Johnson once said, "It is a pity that men and women of God go to bed night after night with no blood on their swords."[2] In his analogy, the "blood on our sword" is the work the believer is involved in each day—healing the sick, preaching the gospel, raising the dead, or simply acting out of kindness in the Name of the Lord.

When we wield our sword, we actively demonstrate to others that the Kingdom of God has come to invade their present circumstances. We reveal destiny and release the potential of the greatness of God. We destroy the work of the enemy and release the Kingdom of God. This is the type of "blood" that should be on our swords each night as we go to bed.

In the process of making your Scripture book you will learn the beauty and intimacy of God, for He is the One who has known you since before you were born. As you seek His face and His presence, you will experientially come to an understanding of the wisdom of God that has been waiting to be revealed in you. Your diligence in this endeavor will benefit you in whatever stage of your walk with God you are in because the increase of His Kingdom and the increase of His government are without end (see Isa. 9:6-7).

God desires that your ear be tuned to Him and that the whisper of His voice be heard and understood by you, His child, the love of His heart. He wants you to come into that place of standing in His presence and speaking to the wind, where you will see what no eye has seen and hear what no ear has heard before. It is in this place that His mysteries are unveiled. This is the doorway to the journey of Scripture book writing.

## USING YOUR BOOK FOR GOD'S GLORY

In creating a Scripture book, we are in the process of creating something for God's glory. We can all be tempted to take the easy way out to get a quick end result by using those Scriptures that are familiar to us and easy to find in the Bible. But understand it is not about filling up a notebook with Bible verses. It is about hearing the whispers of God that have life in them, whispers that can transform the heart. Like everything else in the Christian faith, there is no power in the form. The power rests in God, who transforms our hearts and our lives.

We must use our Scripture books in order to understand the value of them. It was not until I created my fourth book that I began to experience this special place with God. The first few books I created were like the process of digging ore for a sword—each book was part of the process of honing a living sword within me. When I first began, in my haste to complete the task and flesh out the revelation, I simply put in Scriptures I had previously memorized, categorizing them like a concordance. But at the end of six months I felt something was missing. I didn't understand that I needed to listen to the whispers of God as part of the creative process.

Don't be tempted to fill up your book quickly. Wait for those heavenly whispers that come from above. You are aiming to go beyond the written Word into the *living* Word of God.

Unless you are built up in your own faith and walking with God you are not going to have the "overflow" to provide life-giving ministry to others. You will be able to give an opinion but not the life that God offers through His living Word. He desires that we give the Word of truth that goes forth in power, gentleness, and correction, producing life and accomplishing what it was sent to do.

All truth you have yet to obtain. Sure, you have a measure of truth and you have truth about certain things. But you do not possess the sum of all truth. Remember, you can't give away what you do not own. We often deny the things that we have not experienced simply because we have never experienced them. But just because something does not exist in your life does not mean it does not exist at all.

The Word coming alive in you is what you give to your experiential life so that it can catch up with your revelatory life. The living Word *in* you is ministry. Your Scripture book will be filled with affirmations based on what you have experienced in your time with God.

## GETTING STARTED

As you hear God's whispers and Scriptures come into your heart, categorize them in ways that relate to your world, your life, and then to your ministry—that particular area of influence God has you in, in the present moment. Please remember that every category you select for your Scripture book should be specific to *your* life and ministry. Here are some suggested categories to help get you started. You won't necessarily come up with the same categories that I have. These categories are only suggestions to get you started.

- Angels

- Anger

- Anointing

- Answered Prayer and Prayer Requests

- Authority

- Baptism (Water, Holy Spirit, and Fire)

- Covenant Promises of God

- Demons

- Depression

- Destiny

- Dreams

- Faith

- Fear

- Finances (Tithing and Giving)

- Glory of God

- Healing

- Hearing God

- Holy Spirit

- Humility

- Kindness

- Kingdom

- Living Word

- Lordship

- Mercy

- Parenting and Children

- Power

- Power of the Tongue

- Prayer and Intercession

- Renewed Mind: To renew the mind we must live differently, not just think differently.

- Revelation Nuggets (for Me)

- Salvation

- Temple of God

- Test and Trials

- Visions

- Worship

There are many places and ways to receive Scriptures and revelatory thoughts for your book. Here is my list. It is not comprehensive, but it includes some of the major ways you can receive from God:

- From your own study of the Bible

- In articles that expound on Scripture as you receive insight to that particular message

- During times of prayer

- In books you read as illumination comes from certain Scriptures about which the author is writing

- Through conversations with others

- From sermons that inspire truth to your spirit

- In dreams and visions

- Through worship

- In life

My husband and I were hiking in North Carolina and Tennessee some time ago. While in a state park, we decided to take the horse trails rather than the hiking trail. At one point we got off the trail and followed a stream to the top. When we did, we found three gravestones beside the trail. It was a tender moment to think about those who had come before us. We couldn't help but wonder when was the last time someone had been along this trail. Had anyone hiked here since these people were laid in their graves? It was such an obscure location, with no town nearby, only hundreds of miles of park in every direction. We told the rangers of our discovery, but they had no record of the graves. It is possible that we were the first to discover them since these dear ones died. When we made the decision to step off the beaten path and blaze our own trail, we discovered things unknown.

That is how it should be with your Scripture book. Don't take the familiar path with Scriptures that you know well. Listen for the whispers of God, and discover the unknown. Once you begin to earnestly seek God's living sword within you, you will find that God has been trying to do this all along; you just didn't realize it. Your Scripture book will become the tool that illuminates His revelation.

There is no shortcut in experiencing God. Keep it simple, and the complex will be revealed. As you create multiple Scripture books, your experience with God will get defined and refined, and you will find that subsequent books get richer.

## HANDWRITING VERSUS TYPING

I have often had people ask if they should handwrite their Scripture book or type it. From personal experience and from testimonies of others who have used this tool, handwriting takes the greater commitment and brings the greater reward.

For those of you who are addicted to your computer it will be hard not to use it for this process. For you to be alone with your pen, God, and your Bible will be a challenge in itself. You may have to start by handwriting your Scriptures and then sit down at the computer to type out your revelatory thoughts as you create your book. The two do go hand in hand, and often the revelation comes so quickly it is hard to write by hand. But still I urge you to handwrite the Scriptures, at least for your first few books.

In ancient times of first kings, if they were to make a law or ruling, they had to take pen to parchment themselves because what they wrote affected the entire kingdom. Think of handwriting as the covenant or contract you are making with every person who will ever be in your life. And the responsibility to put down the tablet or computer and handwrite has a key that unveils what typing cannot do.

Here is a testimony toward that: I have a dear friend, and he has an almost photographic memory. When he was praying about the assignment I had given in church to handwrite Scripture books, he wrestled with God about the need to do so because of his gift. But the Lord spoke very clearly: the assignment was to handwrite. He said the most amazing experience came over him when he sat down to write the Scripture. It was an intimacy he had not previously explored. He then encouraged me to write a book concerning the process, for it was so transforming.

The fruit is in the journey, not the destination itself. Remember, it is not your goal just to fill a book; the goal is to experience God and His living Word in your heart and life.

You can use your later drafts to cut and paste for study and book writing, or sermon notes, letters, and e-mails, and for social media, as a way to encourage others.

At this point you should have some solid ideas of how to go about creating your own Scripture book. And you should know the importance of categorizing the Scriptures in ways that are meaningful to you. Now it is time to turn our attention to the ways in which God can make His Word come alive in your life as you use your Scripture books. This is where true transformation takes place.

## NOTES

1.  Bill Johnson, Voice of the Apostles Conference, Harrisburg, PA, 2005.

2.  Bill Johnson, *Leadership Advance, Bethel Church, Redding, CA, 2006.*

## Chapter 3

# THE TRANSFORMATION IN USING THE BOOK

*For just as the body without the spirit is dead,*
*so also faith without works is dead.*

—JAMES 2:26

## THE NORMAL CHRISTIAN LIFE

John Wimber was a great man of God with an apostolic voice for his time. His ministry had a global effect on modern Christianity. Even today, years after his passing, the ripple effects of his life, teachings, and experiences on the wider Body of Christ are evident internationally. In his life he contended for the message of the Kingdom of God, not religion. We, the Church, are the beneficiaries of his inheritance. He taught us by word and example—through invitation, impartation, and demonstration—how to experience the passionate love of God through the movement of the Holy Spirit.

John used to say by way of sincere invitation, "Come, Holy Spirit," and God would show up in a powerful and tangible way. Those of us present would see the Spirit of God pull back the veil of our blindness and show us what He was doing. We learned firsthand from the Holy Spirit. We witnessed various manifestations, including deliverances and healings. The supernatural became evident as the gateway of heaven opened. The work of the enemy was bound and the blessings of heaven poured out.

John's passing was a loss to the Church globally. His life was an example of a heart given over to worship and to a passion for the Father. He had compassion for the fatherless and a love for God, which he expressed with all his strength. His resolve was to speak with the deepest wisdom of God, and to impart to the Body of Christ what he was given. It was a privilege to live and witness the life and ministry of John Wimber first-hand. I love John and all that he has meant to my family and myself. Even today, the anointing is still so fresh through his books. Some of my favorites are *Power Evangelism*, *Power Healing*, and *Kingdom Mercy*.[1]

His practical, down-to-earth teachings and profound moments of truth all blended together in one man. One of my favorite sayings of his is, "I'm just a fat man trying to get to heaven." He was humble, but his journey blazed a trail for so many of us to walk into the presence of God and to find Him to be not an angry God but a loving Father.

## SEEING HEAVEN INVADE EARTH

Bill Johnson is another apostolic voice in our time who is influencing the Church globally in a way very similar to John Wimber. He teaches that the Kingdom of God is in the here and now, invading our present reality. Like John Wimber, Bill is a prolific author. Some of my favorite books by Bill are *When Heaven Invades Earth, The Supernatural Power of a Transformed Mind, Dreaming With God,* and *Strengthen Yourself In The Lord.*[2] Each of these books expounds on the binding and loosing of the Kingdom of God in the realm of the present, showing believers how to walk out the experiential Kingdom life.

In *When Heaven Invades Earth,* Bill writes:

We were born to rule—rule over creation, over darkness—to plunder hell and establish the rule of Jesus wherever we go by preaching the gospel of the Kingdom. Kingdom means: King's domain. In the original purpose of God, mankind ruled over creation. Now that sin has entered the world, creation has been infected by darkness, namely: disease, sickness, afflicting spirits, poverty, natural disasters, demonic influence, etc. Our rule is still over creation, but now it is focused on exposing and undoing the works of the devil. We are to give what we have received to reach that end. If I truly received power from an encounter with the God of power, I am equipped to give it away. The invasion of God into impossible situations comes through a people who have received power from on high and learn to release it into the circumstances of life.[3]

Our spirits are searching to understand. When we appropriate God's understanding, it will enable us to see, comprehend, and enlarge our life-grid. The question that begs to be asked is, "Have you seen yet?"

Christopher Columbus was in the Caribbean with his clipper ships anchored offshore for several days before the native tribes could see them. Were they invisible? No. But the natives had no reality-grid in their minds for an object like a clipper ship. The shaman could see the effect of the boat in the water and wondered what was causing it. Each day he would stand on the shore and look out, until one day his mind could comprehend this new experiential reality and translate it to the actual revealed reality of the ships. As he described the ships to the other tribesmen, they could then see the ships, too. But it was only because of their faith in the shaman and trust of what he saw that their eyes were opened to see.

Remember the movie *Field of Dreams*?[4] Kevin Costner's character hears the phrase, "If you build it, he will come." So he builds a baseball field and then he keeps getting keys to a new experienced reality. Soon his wife, daughter, and James Earl Jones's character can all see, hear, smell, touch, and taste a new reality to which others were blind, including his brother-in-law. Then, at the end of the movie, we see the line of cars beginning to wind down the road to come and see. It is a Hollywood example of "there is more"—more than we are aware of in this visible realm. It is the deep stirring in each of us to know and be known, to seek that which is greater, and to be part of that reality. As the Psalmist said, "Deep calls to deep..." (Psalm 42:7).

We must experience and not just know about the Kingdom of God. As we begin to get acquainted with the Kingdom, we learn to speak the truth of that Kingdom, which is out "there," into the here and now. We release heaven into the earth as we learn the glories of His Kingdom and begin to understand our great need to know and proclaim the Word of God over our life and situation. This written and living Word of God is the greatest truth. It has the power to change our hearts and our circumstances. Its effect is deeper than our intellectual understanding can even begin to conceive.

## SHADOWS OF HIS KINGDOM

One of the most stirring movies for me personally was *The Matrix*.[5] I was so overwhelmed with all the types and shadows of the Kingdom of God and the mind-numbing reality of the sin and poverty into which we are born. I was also reminded of the captivity that people suffer and how complete it is in its deception. People suffer without realizing there is a Savior and an intimate relationship with their Creator that pulls us from captivity to freedom.

After I saw *The Matrix*, I took the leadership of our church to see it and had a discussion of the images the Wachowski brothers placed in the movie. I then wrote sixteen pages about the types and shadows of the Kingdom of God that were obvious to me from the movie. The voice of God was crying out to me, and I openly wept with conviction for a lost and dying world.

A teacher friend of ours in Austria used these sixteen pages about types and shadows in his high school humanities classroom as a topic of discussion. Several teenagers from his classroom came to Christ as a result. My simple response of compassion to a movie and a few hours of labor and writing brought people to a saving knowledge of Jesus Christ. Isn't this a perfect reminder of how God created us to know His heart for a lost and dying world and to release the truth of His Kingdom?

We are born for more than what we see present in the natural. Our spiritual DNA cries out for more; that is why we are at unrest, why we feel the nagging in our soul that nothing in this world can satisfy. That is why we push the envelope, the cutting edge of life—to drink in more experience, to know more.

## PRAYING THE WORD OF GOD

Michael and I were a part of the Word of Faith movement at one point in our lives. When we moved on to pursue other demonstrations of the Kingdom, we choose not to "throw the baby out with the bathwater" when it came to what we learned in the Word of Faith movement. The foundational roots of our passionate love of the Word of God grew tremendously while we were there. We came to understand the authority of the Word of God and why it must be in our heart at all times. We learned why it is that God is moved by the economy of faith we place in His Word, because it is by faith that the Kingdom may be made evident.

We became part of the Vineyard movement in the 1980s, where we learned about power evangelism, the prophetic voice of the Church, and how to pursue healing past wounds in people's hearts. It was in the Vineyard that we learned in a deeper way to pray the Word of God, which is always the factor that makes the difference and often turns the tide in any particular situation.

I have grown to appreciate a quote found in a secular book entitled *Rogue Warrior* by Richard Marcinko, a former Navy Seal, and John Weisman. Marcinko repeats a motto the Navy Seals often use: "The more you sweat in training, the less you bleed in combat."[6] There are so many times in our life when we do not have the knowledge to quote Scripture to fight back against the enemy. Or we have been trapped by our circumstances or overwhelmed by emotion during a particular season and we cannot focus long enough to get into Scripture. It is at these times that I find my

Scripture books to be a great help to me. I can turn to the category that I need, or when I'm praying for someone, I can quickly find the Scripture needed and begin to pray the Scripture into that particular situation. There are many reasons to do this. Here are just a few:

- As a reminder of how big God is.

- To draw the line in the sand so the enemy will not prevail. Remember, "submit therefore to God. Resist the devil and he will flee from you" (James 4:7).

- To put the covenant out again, for "the prayer of [the] righteous man [will] accomplish much" (James 5:16).

- To give the angels something to perform (see Ps. 103:20).

- God is watching over His Word to perform it: "You have seen well, for I am watching over My word to perform it" (Jeremiah 1:12).

- To show that His Word will not return void and come back without accomplishing that which it was meant to do (see Isa. 55:10-11).

- Because He is Jehovah: "the Alpha and the Omega...who is and who was and who is to come, the Almighty" (Revelation 1:8).

- For you may search the Scriptures, and think that you are finding eternal life; but these are they that testify of Me (see John 5:39).

*"As for Me, this is My covenant with them,"* *says the Lord: "My Spirit which is upon you,* *and My words which I have put in your mouth* *shall not depart from your mouth, nor from the* *mouth of your offspring, nor from the mouth of* *your offspring's offspring," says the Lord, "from* *now and forever"* (Isaiah 59:21).

*I have put My words in your mouth and have* *covered you with the shadow of My hand, to* *establish the heavens, to found the earth, and* *to say to Zion, "You are My people."* (Isaiah 51:16).

*This book of the law shall not depart from your* *mouth, but you shall meditate on it day and* *night, so that you may be careful to do accord-* *ing to all that is written in it; for then you will* *make your way prosperous, and then you will* *have success* (Joshua 1:8).

## SPEAKING PRODUCES ACTION

Reading and writing the Scriptures makes a way for the "doing"—for the actual practice of the Scriptures in our everyday life. Speaking is doing. As we speak out and write down the Scriptures, they become part of us, transforming us into a living sword to be used for God's glory. Speaking the Word of God with our mouth produces and strengthens the Word of God in our heart.

Remember that each of these Scriptures states that the Word of God is to be in our mouth and to be spoken by us on a continual basis. It is not something we are only to read in the morning, and then go on with our day. The Word of God is to become part of us, to be on our lips and proclaimed by us.

We must put feet to wisdom, and wisdom to understanding, because true understanding is experiential. And experiential understanding will breathe wisdom into our life because experiential understanding is the road of spiritual maturation.

Revival or reformation can often be stalled because we are not *doing* the Word of God. We must be doers of the Word and not only hearers. Without doing, the Body of Christ is in the process of stalling another renewal. As individuals, we are often timid and unwilling to ask people if they would like prayer. Our reluctance holds us back from partnering with God to invade the earth with His Kingdom. In the process, we can hold others back from receiving their miracle. In these kinds of circumstances, all we need to do is pray to God and trust that He will do the work. Jesus said, "But the Father abiding in Me does His works" (John 14:10).

## DEAD IN CHRIST

Our lives cannot be hid in Christ with God until we are fully dead to self. The resurrection power comes after we are of no reputation and can fully comprehend our death and resurrection in the baptismal tank. For Paul said:

> *Or do you not know that all of us who have been baptized into Christ Jesus have been baptized into His death? Therefore we have been buried with Him through baptism into death, so that as Christ was raised from the dead through the glory of the Father, so we too might walk in newness of life. For if we have become united with Him in the likeness of His death, certainly we shall also be in the likeness of His resurrection, knowing this, that our old self was crucified with Him, in order that our body of sin might be done away with, so that we would no longer be slaves to sin; for he who has died is freed from sin* (Romans 6:3-7).

Then he goes on to say:

> *What benefit did you reap at the time from the things you are now ashamed of? Those things result in death! But now that you have been set free from sin and have become slaves of God, the benefit you reap leads to holiness, and the result is eternal life. For the wages of sin is death, but the gift of God is eternal life in Christ Jesus our Lord* (Romans 6:21-23 NIV).

We often don't know how to pray or even what we should pray for. Because of this, we should simply choose to pray the highest prayer available, which is praying the Word of God, the Scriptures. Pray in the Spirit, and the Spirit will illuminate to you the difference between the prayer of petition, the prayer of declaration, prayers of intercession that give us an open heaven, and prayers that avail much. If your prayer life has stopped or lost momentum, all you need to do is add to it the Scriptures from your book and new life will come again. The Word works!

Prayer and revelation are meant to bring us into an encounter with God. Without an encounter we have only refined our religion. Revelation is not just to increase our head knowledge; that is automatic when embraced with a humble heart. Revelation is to bring empowerment and to reestablish our authority in Christ and His Word.

As you create your Scripture book, the Word of God will be internalized in your heart. This process of meditation produces action so that you can become *doers* of God's Word, speaking it out. Creating Scripture books is a wonderful way to let God's Word come alive in your heart, producing action in your life.

## NOTES

1.  John Wimber and Kevin Springer, *Power Evangelism* (Ventura, CA: Regal Books, 1986, 2009); John Wimber and Kevin Springer, *Power Healing* (San Francisco, CA: Harper, 1987); John Wimber and Kevin Springer, *Kingdom Mercy* (London: Hodder & Stoughton, 1988).

2.  Bill Johnson, *When Heaven Invades Earth* (Shippensburg, PA: Destiny Image, 2003); Bill Johnson, *The Supernatural Power of a Transformed Mind* (Shippensburg, PA: Destiny Image, 2005); Bill Johnson, *Dreaming with God: Secrets to Redesigning Your World Through God's Creative Flow* (Shippensburg, PA: Destiny Image, 2006); Bill Johnson, *Strengthen Yourself in the Lord: How to Release the Hidden Power of God in Your Life* (Shippensburg, PA: Destiny Image, 2007).

3.  Johnson, *When Heaven Invades Earth*, 32-33.

4.  *Field of Dreams*, directed by Phil Alden Robinson (1989; Universal City, CA: Universal Pictures, 1998), DVD.

5.  *The Matrix*, directed by Andy and Lana Wachowski (1999; Burbank, CA: Warner Home Video, 1999), DVD.

6.  Richard and John Weisman, *Rogue Warrior* (New York: Pocket Books, 1998).

## Chapter 4

# AS A WEAPON OF INTERCESSION

*Now therefore, O Lord God, the word that You have
spoken concerning Your servant and his house, confirm
it forever, and do as You have spoken, that Your name
may be magnified forever, by saying, "The Lord of hosts
is God over Israel"; and may the house of Your servant
David be established before You. For You, O Lord of
hosts, the God of Israel, have made a revelation to Your
servant, saying, "I will build you a house"; therefore Your
servant has found courage to pray this prayer to You.*

—2 SAMUEL 7:25-27

*And when they had prayed, the place where
they had gathered together was shaken, and they
were all filled with the Holy Spirit and began
to speak the word of God with boldness.*

—ACTS 4:31

## SCRIPTURE BECOMES A WEAPON

I have been developing Scripture books for many
years, and I want to reiterate Richard Marcinko's

words: "The more you sweat in training, the less you bleed in combat," because it is such an important concept in the life of the believer.[1] In the instant we need to fight, we will not have time to look up Scriptures with which to fight. The continued exercise of writing and reading my Scripture books has resulted in less blood on the battlefield for me, and I know it will for you, too.

The first year I made a Scripture book, we were in our weekly Bible study one evening when the phone rang. I answered the call to hear a woman from a church in the Boston area tell me that her nephew was in a local hospital with a possible brain aneurism. Her sister and family were nearby on vacation visiting their parents when the son fell over in the living room after swimming. He was now at the hospital. She was calling for our church to pray for the healing of this boy.

I quickly went to the front room and told everyone, and the typical prayer model went forth with agreement from the others. By typical I mean that one person prayed (me) while the rest listened and said, "Yes, Lord" and "amen." Then they went back to the Bible study like that was enough And on one level that is true.

However, I could not go back to the Bible study because a weapon of force and power was activated inside of me. It broke the model and pushed me forward to what were uncharted territories at the time. I could hear Scriptures going off in my spirit, one after another. I went to the bedroom and grabbed my Scripture book, turned to my section on healing, and began to declare with authority and faith that this boy would live and not die. I prayed Scripture after Scripture, saying the child's name on his behalf and releasing the authority of heaven to preempt the circumstances. I turned to my section on the promises of God and prayed those Scriptures as well. I prayed in tongues until I had higher revelation and then started praying my Scripture book again. This is consistent with the apostle Paul's example when he said, "I will pray with the spirit and I will pray with the mind also" (1 Corinthians 14:15).

I felt the power of God in my voice as I continued to pray. I felt the Kingdom ripple with His power as authority flowed through me. I was experiencing all of this in the bedroom and backyard as the Bible study continued inside my home. As I prayed, I began to see him healed—no memory loss and no infirmity. I saw him whole.

I went to the hospital the next day and introduced myself to the family. They were a Catholic family that did not rightly understand the Word of God or divine healing, but because of their sister, they allowed me to come and pray over their son in the ICU. I went to the hospital every afternoon or evening after I had left work to pray for the child. I wrote Scripture notes and left them for his parents. I laid hands on him and prayed for him again and again. I massaged his arms, hands, legs, and feet when I was there, quoting the Word of God as I touched him. This child was in a coma for four months and left our area to return to Boston in a coma.

I knew that his condition was not the image God had placed in my heart that first night as I prayed. I recalled the day I walked into the room and saw that his arms and legs had begun to show signs of atrophy. His eyes were open, but it seemed as if he wasn't really there. I recalled what God revealed to me the first night in intercession, and where my Scripture book had led me—seeing him with no memory loss, but whole. I stood next to the bed and declared I would not be moved by what I saw or by what the doctor's prognosis was. I declared that he would not be a vegetable. What God had declared and what His Word had spoken were greater in my heart than what I was presently looking at.

Several times the mother called to give me updates of her son's condition. With a tear-soaked voice she would ask me if it was ever going to be any different. I told her one morning that I didn't know how to place in her what was in my heart and mind but I knew her son would wake up and there would be no memory loss. I told her I saw him playing baseball one day and she was to keep praying over him the Scriptures I wrote down.

A few days after Mother's Day I received a telephone call from his mother. She told me she was praying one of the prayers I had written, which she had posted above his bed, and when she misquoted the prayer, he corrected her! He woke from his coma on Mother's Day and knew the Word of God through the prayers that had been continually prayed over him. That is amazing! The Word really works.

That testimony means so much to me because I lived it. But it means so much more to the boy and his family who became believers through the experience. The Word of God healed so much more than just his physical body. The family came and gave their testimony in our church, and this boy walked down the center aisle to the front of our church! His healing had taken place over time. It was not an instantaneous miracle; it was a healing. Healing is often a gradual process, not an instant event.

We knew that hundreds of people were praying for this boy and his family, and through this experience we learned what it means to invest in healing and be a warrior on the battlefield for others. I was trained and transformed in the process. I went from the typical stereotype of someone who prays for others to a warrior intercessor. The Word did that in me—it erupted and powered passion for months of prayer for this child and his family. I was transformed into a Word weapon, with a new level of intercession birthed within me.

## AN IMAGE FORMS FROM THE WORD

In the midst of my initial intercession, as I prayed the Word over this boy, I was given a revelation of the

Kingdom. I felt God's power go forth, and when it did, it placed an image in me of this child fully recovered, with no memory loss or loss of body function. Armed with this revelatory image from God, I was able to stand in prayer for his full recovery, even though circumstances in the natural were contradicting the revelation God had given me. Intercession with the Word of God had revealed His truth, and it was only a matter of time before this boy's condition in the natural caught up with the reality of God's Kingdom in his life. The enemy was defeated, and oh how sweet was the victory of the Lord in the life of this family.

This truth of "seeing" in the spiritual before the answer manifests in the natural is foundational to God's Kingdom invading the earth. Remember Abram? God changed his name to Abraham, meaning "father of multitudes or nations" (see Gen. 17:5). This took place long *before* Abram and Sarah had a son. Remember Jericho? God told Joshua, "See, I have given you the city" (see Josh. 8:1). And this was *before* the walls tumbled down. Remember Gideon? The angel called the frightened Gideon a "mighty man of valor" *before* Gideon and his three hundred men defeated the enemy (see Judg. 6:12). Remember Peter? Jesus said he was the Rock *before* Pentecost (see Matt. 16:18). Remember the Church? Jesus said that we are the light of the world (see Matt. 5:14).

It is fundamental for you "to see" what God has promised you and to stand in faith on His Word to you until it literally changes and transforms the physical realm to conform to His promises. Abraham and Sarah had Isaac, Jericho was conquered, and Peter preached to the multitudes on the day of Pentecost. God's Word is sure and will be established as we stand in agreement with His promises.

## REVELATION BREEDS INTERCESSION

Before you add Scriptures to your book, remember it is important that the Scriptures you choose have revelation for *you*. They must be forged within you in the midst of relationship with God. This is so important. Let me share a story to illustrate this point.

We live in South Florida, where the drivers are horrendous. The roads are not a safe place for beginners. Because of this, when our son turned thirteen, we allowed him to start driving our car in parking lots. We wanted him to have a good feel for the car before he actually began driving on the roads. This turned out to be a good strategy. When he got his license, he was a good driver.

One day he and some friends took our car to a ball game after school. He was driving in the right lane, with a large semi-truck at the stoplight in the center lane ahead of him on a six-lane street. The light turned just as he reached the back of the truck. He let off the brakes and began to accelerate again, going about 15-20 mph. Just as he got to the front of the truck, a boy riding a bike across all six lanes ran into the front of our son's car. He was totally in our son's blind spot because of the location of the truck. The boy on the bike went flying fifteen feet in the air, and when he came down, his head hit the hood of the car and then the pavement. Our son jumped out of his car, ran to the boy, called 911, and then called our house—which was located about ten blocks away.

Our daughter answered the phone and came running from the house to get me. I was pressure-washing the driveway. As she ran to the car, I heard her yell that there had been an accident and the boy who was hit was not moving. I dropped the pressure washer and ran to our car with words flowing from my mouth based on Scriptures from my book: "You will live and not die. I place you under the covenant of the blood of Jesus. I claim you as my child. You will have the blessings and covering of my home and the blood of Jesus."

My daughter and I jumped in the car and raced to the scene. I ran to my son, saw he was physically okay, then ran to the injured boy all the while quoting Scripture and speaking the promises of God over him. I prayed that the paramedics would not miss anything, that all things would be revealed to them, and that they would be led by the wisdom and the anointing of God. I continued to speak to the injured child, telling him that he was under the covering of my house as my son through spiritual adoption. The paramedics, thinking I was his mother because they heard me claiming him as my son, pushed everyone back except me. When it came time to get him into the helicopter, they tried to get me to get in too. I had to explain that I didn't know the child, that I was just interceding for his life.

My husband and our other daughter were at the scene by this time, trying to comfort our son, who was very distraught. There were several eyewitnesses, including an off-duty police officer, who said the boy, thinking it was safe to cross because all the cars were stopped, just ignored the light. Of course it is always the unforeseen that snares our life.

We continued to pray as the helicopter roared off to the hospital. According to a friend who was at work at the hospital that particular day, the boy was given only two hours to live when he arrived. But our intercession, and the intercession of all the people we called, began to go up to heaven and fill the altar before the throne and invade the territory of the enemy. Once again, the Scripture book was my weapon. My Scriptures were there for me, and as I prayed them, the life and power of God's Word went forth to stop death and release healing.

As the weeks went by, we continued to pray for this boy and his family. If you have ever done this kind of intercession, I am sure you have noticed how your mind and emotions can get weary in a situation like this. After a while, everything tells you to quit. You start to think that perhaps the lack of healing is the will of God. Others around you who have been trained to pray only once as a demonstration of faith begin to make you feel like perhaps your continued prayers are a sign of unbelief. In these situations, I have found that perseverance in speaking the Word of God *is* faith and that I am in the glorious position to co-labor with God. I have learned never to let thoughts of quitting enter my heart or mind until I get my answer from God. My fallback position in the face of quitting is to say, "NO!" The Word of God is the will of God, and I will settle for nothing else to my last breath.

After several months, this boy totally recovered! He now plays sports and has a normal life. Death intended to take him and to steal my son's well-being in the process. The enemy's strategy was thwarted by the power of the Word of God proclaimed from our lips.

I know the Word will always accomplish its purposes. I know it was the hard work of creating Scripture books that put that Word in my mouth and sealed it in my heart, enabling the proclamations to go forth with power. What was meant for evil, God turned to His good.

Now you can see why I stress that it is in the sweat of training that less blood is spilled on the battlefield. In the midst of crisis, we will not have time to grab a Bible and look up healing Scriptures. They must have been forged within us. The first time I wielded the Word of God in intercession for the boy in a coma, God was still in the process of forging His sword in me. By the second time, in the midst of a life-and-death situation, the

Scriptures were part of my being and resulted in God's authority over the situation. As it poured out of me in the midst of battle, God's Word flooded the scene, bringing change and transformation. Remember, "the effective prayer of a righteous man can accomplish much" (James 5:16).

## GOD TRAINS YOU FOR BATTLE

I take my Scripture books with me to other countries when I minister. I find that when I am in the intercession room, the Spirit of God leads me to pray certain categories of Scripture over people and churches, cities, and sometimes the whole land. The anointing released through this process is an experience I have yet to be able to describe, except to say I have glimpsed things I thought were reserved only for prophets of old.

The more you use the books you create, the more you will find that God uses them to train you to become who you are in Christ. Your heart cry will be heard and answered as He lives in you and brings the things of His Kingdom into the desires of your heart.

God used my Scripture books several times in Brazil as I interceded over cities. I remember the time He gave a word of knowledge for a particular city. He told me where the bones of witches and witchdoctors had been placed in specific marker points throughout the country, sending a curse over the entire country. Using my Scripture book, I went to the categories of

"Authority Over Demons" and "Covenant Promises." Armed with these Scriptures, the intercessory team and I began to pray to break the curses on those bones and the strongholds of territories of the enemy over that city. The authority of God was present in us to bind the work of the enemy, breaking the power of the curses contained in those bones. The call of God for that city was released through our intercession. We witnessed the power of the Word bring victory for the Kingdom of God. We saw thousands of deliverances and healings in the meetings after this time of intercession. The ministry team was exhausted by the time we left the city.

The key was in the power of the Scripture, revealed through the Scripture book, and in those of us willing to pray the Word. Remember Jesus' parable of the widow and the unjust judge? Luke says the parable was told in order that we should "pray and not...lose heart" (Luke 18:1). The Greek understanding of that phrase means "to not cave in" or "to not shrink back."

> *And the Lord said, "Hear what the unrighteous judge said; now, will not God bring about justice for His elect who cry to Him day and night, and will He delay long over them? I tell you that He will bring about justice for them quickly. However, when the Son of Man comes, will He find faith on the earth?"* (Luke 18:6-8)

The Word of God in your heart and on your lips can be used as a powerful weapon of intercession. God will use you when you least expect it because you have become the living sword of the Lord by His power.

## NOTE

1.  Marcinko and Weisman, *Rogue Warrior,* 32.

## Chapter 5

# BUILDING YOUR FAITH

*And He summoned the twelve and began to send them out
in pairs, and gave them authority over the unclean spirits.*

—MARK 6:7

*They went out and preached that men should repent.
And they were casting out many demons and were
anointing with oil many sick people and healing them.*

—MARK 6:12-13

*The apostles gathered together with Jesus; and they
reported to Him all that they had done and taught.*

—MARK 6:30

## WHERE DID HIS AUTHORITY COME FROM?

On a mission trip to Brazil, as I sat with thousands
of others listening to a man of God teach, the fresh-
ness of his teaching accompanied by the stirring of
the Holy Spirit came over me. He was teaching on a
subject on which I had taught several times before.
Some of the phrasing was different, but I knew I had

taught that same truth. And I remembered that when I had taught that lesson, the congregation, moved by the Spirit of God, had experienced a great ministry time afterwards. How was it that my spirit was being so stirred upon hearing this lesson again?

I believe it was stirred by the authority of the man teaching. He carried a fresh authority. When those of us in ministry teach, we teach from the Scriptures, bringing encouragement to the Body. The life we give to others through the Scriptures comes from the same source, from the Word of God inspired by the Holy Spirit. We have different methods of delivery but the same source of truth. Let me give you a few of the different ways that Kingdom life is communicated and Kingdom authority imparted:

- **One:** What we hear others teach comes alive in us so that we can believe it. And as we believe it, we study it so that we may pass it on to others.

- **Two:** It comes through personal revelation, given to us by the Holy Spirit, that we dig from the Word of God for ourselves.

- **Three:** It comes from experiential knowledge as we live out His revelations in our daily lives.

- **Four:** It comes through practicing what we believe, and in the process having revelation rooted in us.

- **Five:** It is evident in the increased authority in us, as the "old man" falls away and the Kingdom of God is displayed in our lives.

Both revelation and living out the revelation are examples of truth, and both will result in ministry; but the latter is far more empowered than the former.

Each step of release has power because His truth sets us free. If I don't give away what I have, have I truly begun to own it? I believe that we must own something in order to give it away. As soon as a truth is revealed to my spirit, I have to go find someone with whom to share it. It is in this way that I claim ownership of that freshly revealed truth. Then I must with diligence invest it in my life and behavior.

## THE KEY TO ABSOLUTE RESOLVE

Deuteronomy 29:29 says, "The secret things belong to the Lord our God, but the things revealed belong to us and to our sons forever, that we may observe all the words of this law." If you study that truth, if you put time and pen to this Scripture, then it will take root in your heart and in your spirit. You must begin to put feet to it if you want authority to increase in your life, because when you are a doer of the Word, you experience the power of that particular truth. It now lives in you. And when you release that Word, the authority of heaven backs you up because it has been released in faith and out of experiential knowledge.

When the Word of God creates a heart of absolute resolve in your spirit, your life is elevated to the consciousness of the God of the impossible, with whom there is no limitation, restriction, or inability to create out of nothing.

By the time you have finished creating Scripture books you too will realize the absolute resolve of the Scriptures in you. On the journey of experience you will come to understand that you are bigger inside than the container in which you live or the three dimensions and time to which you're restricted. Will the storms of life be over? Of course they won't. But you will be equipped to have authority, to speak with authority, and to live in the authority of the Kingdom of God.

"How will this happen?" you ask. It will happen as your mind is renewed. Faith comes by hearing (not having heard) the Word of God (see Rom. 10:17). This Scripture is not talking about the physical ears of your head, but the ears of your spirit man being opened. As Jesus would often say, "He who has ears to hear, let him hear" (Matthew 11:15). The washing of the water of the Word cleanses our spiritual ears, allowing us to walk in strength (see Eph. 5:26).

## SOW INTO THE SPIRIT

We are a spirit; we possess a soul and live in a physical body. Through our years of counseling experience we estimate the typical Christian will spend seventy-five percent of daily activity involved in the activities of the body; twenty percent with the activities of the soul (mind, will, and emotions); and five percent on spiritual pursuits.

We all need to sow into the Spirit and to invest in the supernatural realm of God. If there is any activity or discipline that you can do to get those numbers to shift, you will see yourself begin to grow. This is why Paul tells the Galatians to sow to the Spirit:

> *Do not be deceived, God is not mocked; for whatever a man sows, this he will also reap. For the one who sows to his own flesh will from the flesh reap corruption, but the one who sows to the Spirit will from the Spirit reap eternal life* (Galatians 6:7-8).

Here are some points to ponder about what it means to sow in the Spirit:

- **Prayer**—this is not about praying for others or for your circumstances. I am talking about prayer where you spend time with the Father so that it is not about Him performing something for you. This could be where you just connect in deep relationship, where He is the lover of your soul, your Papa, and you just love being with Him. The kind of prayer that develops more than love is one that gets to the crucial element of trusting Him as Papa.

- **Reading and Study**—this is about study only until it moves your spirit. You are to spend time with the Father when you are moved from your study. I am not talking about study for the sake of getting more religious information. You can know every ingredient of a cake and never eat one. We must "taste and see that the Lord is good" (Psalm 34:8). We must experience Him and not just know facts about Him. When He moves you stop, take the time to know what just happened and why.

- **Scripture Book Writing**—this is a great door that, when opened, will release heaven on earth. But if you just do the process and neglect the source of the Word, it will be for naught. If you allow yourself to be the brush that paints the face of the Father for the world and do not see the picture, you will fail to understand God and His Kingdom. You must become the living Word made flesh, dwelling in this world without being part of the world. Intimacy with His Word will develop this ability in you.

- **Fellowship**—this is to be so much more than a time to discuss different topics. We should break the bread of life together, which is involvement in one another's life, using our giftings to call the greatness from one another, advancing the Kingdom of God as He develops destinies.

- **Giving**—we are to put before the Lord of heaven and earth a token upon which we have placed our faith. It is our declaration of His Lordship over all that we know and all over which have been given control. It is an impartation of faith on money or goods. It is offering with destiny placed upon it—a covenant of His Kingdom, where we understand that all provision will always come from Him.

## BUILDING FAITH AND EXPANDING THE KINGDOM

When we understand that spending time intimately with the Word is unlocking the Kingdom, we will be able to build our faith and expand the Kingdom. Faith is belief, and belief is the authority of the Father. He does the work. Jesus said, "He who has seen Me has seen the Father" (John 14:9). It has to be "us and more of Him." The transformation of our mind is a supernatural lifestyle that God has waiting for us.

Bill Johnson writes:

So many of us see the storm and pray the same as the disciples pray when they saw Jesus sleeping in the boat: "Don't You care that we are perishing?" Jesus got up and answered their prayer. Most of us feel good when God answers our prayers. We might even applaud the disciples for doing the right thing in this circumstance, but Jesus turned to them and said, "How *come you don't have any faith?*" *"Wait a minute!" they might have thought, "I had enough faith to come and talk to You! And You did what I asked! I thought I was paid to pray, and you were paid to do!" No, it is our responsibility to command that obstacle to disappear. Most people's ministry involves trying to get God to fix problems on earth when we should be commanding the storms to be calm. We should see situations from heaven's perspective and declare the word of the Lord—and watch heaven invade.*[1]

He goes on to write:

It's because you have divine purpose. He wants you to use the tools He has given you to bring about the "heavenly" result...if you are facing a spiritual battle, it is usually because you have been trained for that moment. It means you have been experiencing things in your life that should have taught you how to respond to the present storm...you should be ready to step in and say, "I believe God for a miracle in this situation. That backslidden child will return home. That disease in your body is broken in the name of Jesus. That financial crisis is over."[2]

He goes on to encourage us that the time to pray and prepare is before the battle, much like Jesus did. Jesus cried out to God in private times when nothing was wrong. That is how He "stored up" His power and created an inner atmosphere of peace and faith that was available when troubling situations arose so that He could face the storm Bill once said, "You can have authority over any storm you can sleep in or have peace in."[3]

Understanding these concepts gives you another tool for the journey of preparation for all your future miracles. Remember, "the more you sweat in training, the less you bleed in combat!"[4]

## A REGULAR CLEANING

We all have areas of life that need to be cleaned on a regular basis, much like the houses in which we live. The same is true of our spiritual walk. Just listening to someone else's problems can put "dirt" in our mind. So do television and conversations that we overhear, not to mention all the other activities in which we are intentional participants. That is why we need to be washed with the water of the Word on a continual basis (see Eph. 5:26).

We are filled with cobwebs from the past. Little spider-like demonic lies are always spinning in our mind and setting new traps for us. No matter how old we are in the Lord or how close our walk with God is, that will never stop. An active war is in process. You and I are in that war whether we like it or not, or whether we even acknowledge it or not. We are servants of God, friends of God, children of God, people of God, and worshipers of God. Anyone who walks as a child of God is in the battle. The battle rages because we are the spotless Bride now! Resurrection and Grace have placed us there.

We get deceived into selling ourselves short on what God has given us, what He is doing with us and through us. We can become enamored of the lives of well-known Christians such as Billy Graham or Kathryn Kuhlman or Smith Wigglesworth and sell ourselves short. That kind of thinking is the enemy's deception to keep us from coming into the fullness of who God created us to be. Live like the Bride: you have His name; you have access to all His currency. Isaiah 61: "The Spirit of the Lord...is upon me" (Isaiah 61:1). To what? What are you taking authority to spend? What are you being deceived into not stepping into?

He has given all things!

## WHAT IS YOUR NAME?

Why do we think we have received God's forgiveness but then live under the shadow of our failure? We live willingly under the guilt and shame of yesterday's bad decisions and think it is humility. We must remember that because Christ has risen from the dead, we are not in our sins (see 1 Cor. 15:17).

We often let bad decisions get us down, and dwell on our shortcomings. We internalize them because we think that if we talk to anyone, they might correct us. We focus on our character problems, and they grow overwhelmingly large in our sight. When we feed them with a mind that is not renewed and the power of agreement comes upon the problem, it is then strengthened and multiplied. The damage is done, our emotions win, and our thought life is horrendous. We are restricted to being a smaller vessel than God destined us to be. We live in the smallness of our name rather the incomprehensible Name of Jesus.

Danny Silk has a great teaching on this in his talk titled "What Is Your Name?"[5] He gives an example of his daughter getting the opportunity to tell some adults to relax the rules at an overnight event for the youth, but she didn't have to tell them who her dad was. She knew all she had to do was say her full name and they would obey her. We often forget who our Dad is and the full identity of our name—"Mrs. Jesus Christ." We need to remember that we are His Bride, the Church.

We resist forgiveness because we don't want to be prideful. Remembering how rotten we are makes us feel like we are being humble. Humility is good, but remembering how rotten we are is actually a subtle form of pride. Yesterday's condemnation keeps us focused on ourselves and not on Jesus.

Doubting God's identity was the original sin. When Adam and Eve doubted the Word of God, they sinned, and the action that followed proved the presence of doubt. Adam doubted that he was already made in the image of God when the serpent tempted him and told him that he could make him "like God" (see Gen. 3:5).

In the wilderness, the devil tempted Jesus when he said, "*If* You are the Son of God..." (Matthew 4:6). The enemy wanted Jesus to doubt His identity. It is the same lie and temptation that was presented to Adam and Eve, and the enemy continually presents it to us as well. If we doubt that God has forgiven our sins, our mind will convince us that we are not loved, that He is not with us and will forsake us.

We so often think we are forsaken when God was there all along but we were blind and could not see, deaf and could not hear. This is because in our small-mindedness we refused to understand that His ways are higher than our ways. We must always remember His ways and thoughts are higher than our ways and thoughts (see Isa. 55:9). He was always there, but we were simply unaware. This is the revelation Jacob received at Bethel. Genesis 28:16 says:

> *Then Jacob awoke from his sleep and said, "Surely the Lord is in this place, and I did not know it"* (Genesis 28:16).

## CLEANING HOUSE EVERY DAY

This is the starting point for understanding that our house must be cleaned every day. Scripture books are a great way of cleaning our life and exposing the lies of the enemy so that we can be continually transformed into Christ's image.

When we are emotionally bound to specific events, especially the past, we fail to advance. Our faith is thwarted, and we are doomed to repeat the lesson over and over again. Our mind begins to meditate day and night on the pain of the event until we completely convince ourselves that there is no other option. Our trust is thrust into our victimization, and we trust the pain and the event more than the true reality, thus sealing our prison. It is sealed until the key of God's Word sets us free.

Does it seem as if I know too much about this subject? I tell you these things as one who has walked from the labyrinth of pain, shame, and despair. The key out of this self-imposed prison was the Scripture that was in my mouth, my heart, my spirit, my hand, my meditation, and my being. As the walls of the labyrinth rose to block my life, I cut them down with a living sword and fresh fire from heaven, which is the spoken Word of God called forth to manifest on my behalf.

The imperishable seed of another realm has been placed in the life-giving source of who you are, which is your spirit. It is the seed of the greater life God has for humanity. Before the foundations of the earth, we were called to be the Bride of the Son of God. We are equipped to be equally yoked with Him in all His glory, returning to the pre-fall state of mankind.

I speculate that before the fall, Adam and Eve used more of their mind than we do now. Consider this: Adam was presented other creatures; intuitively, he either knew their nature and function, and thus named them accordingly, or in the image of God he gave them their nature by naming them. He knew the name of all the stars that sang at evening time. He was able to comprehend enough of God to walk in the cool of the day with the Creator and be a companion to Him (see Gen. 3:8).

Today when the presence of God increases in a meeting or a worship session, people often begin to manifest in all sorts of ways. I love the song "I Can Only Imagine" by Mercy Me. It makes me reflect when I consider all the manifestations I have seen in conferences in the past. There is a physical or emotional response when we begin to align with His presence. The majority of the Body of Christ does not know God when He shows up in corporate settings because they have never been in that place of intimacy in His presence in their solitary times. The mature exposure to the reality of God has got to be in there somewhere, but as a Body we have yet to walk in the fullness of companionship—the fullness of being equally yoked with our Bridegroom, Jesus.

I believe the power of the Holy Spirit is given to illuminate the other four hundred billion bits of information that our five senses are taking in. In fact, the Scriptures tell us to sanctify our senses. In Romans,

Paul tells us to present the members of our body as instruments to God for holiness and righteousness, not unrighteousness (see Rom. 6:13). In the book of Hebrews, we are instructed that the mature man trains his senses (see Heb. 5:14).

We have to do what it takes to renew our minds, to forget the former things and live in the present, in His Kingdom that has come. James tells us to walk in the fullness of the light, for He is "the Father of lights, with whom there is no variation or shifting shadow" (James 1:17). Christ did as He saw the Father do. I want that vision of Christ. I want to put my hand to His reality.

I pray for God to open my eyes on a continual basis. I don't just want to see angels and demons, but I want to see Him—to press into the true experiential knowledge of His beauty and wonder. I don't want to be intellectually satisfied with learning stimuli. I want to "press on so that I may lay hold of that for which also I was laid hold of by Christ Jesus" (Philippians 3:12).

The faith we possess should cause our spirit to hunger. It should expose our spiritual appetite to something more than this world can offer. Even the greatest ministry on earth could not satisfy the longing God placed in your heart when you were born. We were created to enjoy all of what is around us, but it was never meant to satisfy us. Where is that drive to have dominion? Where is that hunger for companionship with the Father to share the great "joy of being" that He placed within us?

Every volume of every library in the world could not contain all that Christ did in the thirty-three years He was on this earth (see John 21:25). This was because He came and reestablished dominion on the earth. Those who were with Him and had an understanding of His mission realized all that was being accomplished. For most of us, our lives could be neatly wrapped up in a little two- or three-volume set, which could be tucked onto a bookshelf somewhere because we have yet to fulfill the promise that is ours. Yet fulfilling our promise is an achievable goal *because* of the promise. We just need to press on to the high calling in Christ Jesus.

I encourage you to use your Scripture books to press into the heavens you have not yet discovered and into the whispers of the Father's voice you have not yet heard. I encourage you to feed the seed of His Word in your life. Don't let it get taken away by lack of action. Build your faith. Build your hunger. Build your need. Build your passion. Build your destiny in God! Become the salt that causes others to thirst after the deep water of God because He alone will satisfy. Become undone in His presence.

## NOTES

1. Johnson, *Transformed Mind*, 102.

2. Ibid., 103-04.

3. Johnson, Voice of the Apostles Conference.

4. Marcinko and Weisman, *Rogue Warrior*, 32.

5. Silk, "What Is Your Name?"

## Chapter 6

# PROPHETIC DIRECTION

*I have manifested Your name to the men whom You gave
Me out of the world; they were Yours and You gave them
to Me, and they have kept Your word. Now they have come
to know that everything You have given Me is from You;
for the words which You gave Me I have given to them;
and they received them and truly understood that I came
forth from You, and they believed that You sent Me.*

—JOHN 17:6-8

## AN EXTENSION OF THE LIVING WORD

By now I pray that you have spent time with the
Lord in intimacy and quiet reflection with His Holy
Spirit guiding you as you craft your Scripture book. If
you have done this, then it is inevitable that a very real
transformation is taking place in you.

In the midst of the process of transformation, you
are becoming an extension of the living Word of God
to others. As Christ is formed in you, you become His
hands, His feet, and with your mouth you speak His

Word. As His presence and His Word transform you, the gifts of the Holy Spirit will begin to operate more clearly through you.

When we spend time with Him, when we gaze upon His glory, we are changed into what we see. Paul said it like this:

> *But we all, with unveiled face, beholding as in a mirror the glory of the Lord, are being transformed into the same image from glory to glory, just as from the Lord, the Spirit* (2 Corinthians 3:18).

And John wrote about the Word becoming flesh this way:

> *In the beginning was the Word, and the Word was with God, and the Word was God.... And the Word became flesh, and dwelt among us, and we saw His glory, glory as of the only begotten from the Father, full of grace and truth* (John 1:1,14).

Transformation occurs as you spend time with the Father and His Word. The more time you spend with Him, the more the Word is engrafted in you and the more Christ is formed in you. This is how the "Word becomes flesh" in you, and as it does, others will begin to see His glory reflected in your life to a greater degree.

Like Moses, your face will shine from being in His presence (see Exod. 34:29-35). And like the simple, uneducated fishermen standing before the Jewish Council after Pentecost, they will recognize that you have been with Jesus (see Acts 4:13).

It is not necessary for you to understand how this occurs. Jesus taught us that we would not understand how the Kingdom of God works. We just need to believe that the transformation is occurring. He said, "The kingdom of God is like a man who casts seed upon the soil; and he goes to bed at night and gets up by day, and the seed sprouts and grows—how, he himself does not know" (Mark 4:26-27).

As the process of transformation progresses in your life, the Holy Spirit will create a reservoir of the water of the Word that He will store in your heart so that you can draw from it and give it to others. The Spirit of God will not have to cause rain to fall inside you before ministry can occur. His living water will pour forth from you with ease. A prophetic word from your mouth will grow from a general exhortation to a clearer word.

You will see how the Word goes forth from your own mouth as exhortation and blessing, setting the captives free and strengthening the weak. Jesus said, "The good man out of the good treasure of his heart brings forth what is good...for his mouth speaks from that which fills his heart" (Luke 6:45).

## GIVING SCRIPTURE AS PROPHECY

When you give a Scripture verse to someone, you are giving the simplest form of prophecy, whereby a brother or sister in Christ receives edification, exhortation, and comfort from the Word of God (see 1 Cor. 14:3). I will often look through my Scripture book while in church or at a conference, see a promise of God, and ask the Father, "Who needs this?" He typically highlights someone to me who is in need of this particular encouragement. I promptly write the Scripture down and share it with that person, confident that God will either use it at that moment or whenever that person happens to run across that card or paper in the future. I am confident that God will use His Word in their life.

God's timing is His, and we are His instruments. We don't see the big picture as God sees it. Perhaps that card or paper will find its way to someone else as the Spirit prompts them to share with another person who is truly in need. His timing is always perfect. The Word of God continues to go forth to accomplish what it was sent to do. We can always be confident that the Word will not return empty, like the river that Ezekiel saw flowing from the Temple: "...everything will live where the river goes" (Ezekiel 47:9). It is a matter of obedience to the promptings of the living Word and the whisperings of the Holy Spirit.

When the Word of God is forged in your heart, it will increase the gift of prophecy, even if this is not your primary gifting. Let me give you an example. A woman in our church had a hard time praying out loud for other people. I noticed as she created her

Scripture book that she began to do what I had been doing. She would make small Scripture cards as a word of encouragement that she could easily hand out to others. She would pray for people, and God would give her a specific Scripture for a specific person. She would write the Scripture on a small index card and give it to that person as her way of praying the Word for them. I still have several she wrote for me. Being obedient to write down these Scriptures and give them away was how God began the process of releasing her to minister to others.

## A RESOURCE OF WATER

I encourage you to understand that the inspired Word of God in you is a tool and resource of living water in the hands of God for others around you, even for strangers in your path. This is the promise of God fulfilled in you and in me—He is turning our desert heart into a stream of water for the thirsty. Remember the words of the prophet, and believe that His Word is for you:

> *The scorched land will become a pool and the thirsty ground springs of water* (Isaiah 35:7).

> *The afflicted and needy are seeking water, but there is none, and their tongue is parched with thirst; I, the Lord, answer them Myself, as the God of Israel I will not forsake them. I will open rivers on the bare heights and springs in the midst*

*of the valleys; I will make the wilderness a pool of water and the dry land fountains of water* (Isaiah 41:17-18).

*They will not hunger or thirst, nor will the scorching heat or sun strike them down; for He who has compassion on them will lead them and will guide them to springs of water* (Isaiah 49:10).

Where are those pools, springs, and fountains that the prophet saw in the Spirit? They are being formed in you. God's well of water springing up to everlasting life is in you, ready to flow from you to satisfy the thirsty all around you. Catch the vision and believe the promise that the Father desires to make you a fountain of water to fulfill this prophecy. It is your destiny. Know that all of God's moments, in time, will intersect with the right people as He chooses.

## CO-LABORING WITH GOD

It is the call of God on every believer to change destiny. We can believe in coincidence or we can operate in divine appointment. Every time I give a Scripture to someone, the Holy Spirit intends to use it in that person's life as an instrument to accomplish God's purposes, and perhaps to pass on to another. One person plants; another waters, but it is God who gives the increase (see 1 Cor. 3:6).

Consider what Bill Johnson has to say about being a co-laborer with God: "Is life sweeping you in the flow of activity or are you a vessel that is ruttered and powered with the Word of God and working the current of time to advance the Kingdom in power as a revivalist and as an empowered child of God?"[1]

The spiritual DNA of the Word will transform your thinking and mindset—not by mere mental assent but by a living, experiential walk with God. You are being fully engaged with all your senses in cooperation with the Holy Spirit, growing in wisdom, understanding, and resolve to fulfill the purposes of God in your life, your church, your city, and your region—even to the uttermost parts of the world.

God is calling forerunners with passion and purpose for these last days, people who walk with absolute resolve-resolve in yourself to become the living Word of God—"a refuge from the wind and a shelter from the storm," a "stream of water" for the thirsty (see Isa. 32:2; 41:17-18).

## PROOF GOD IS SPEAKING

Your Scripture book will also help define and reveal some of the strategies of the call of God upon you and your purpose in life. And more importantly, as you develop and reread your book, you will begin to see and hear the actual prophetic word from the Father to you.

The book in its complete form is a record of the very voice of the Father to you. It reveals who you are and how He sees you, how He knows you, and how you know Him.

This broader visual is empowering, because it helps you to see how heaven sees..

I get intimate instruction from Him as I read my Scripture books. There are days when the Lord will instruct me to pick up the navy blue Scripture book with the frayed corners, or the one with artwork on the front, and read it for the day. He speaks to me with a fresh love and familiar whispers of intimacy that affirm I am His child, a woman of God, and He loves me.

One of my favorite movies is *Highlander*.[2] It is a British-American adventure film about warriors who walked the earth for centuries, never growing old. Their destiny lay in a future gathering of immortals and an epic battle that would take place among them, for "there can only be one." In the movie, the only way to kill an immortal was to cut the opponent's head off with a sword.

Some of the immortals were evil, but others were good and would actually train younger ones in the art of sword fighting. When engaged in combat with one another, at the mortal blow, the accumulated power of the opponent would leave the body of the defeated one and would enter the body of the victor. When the transference of "life force" occurred in the movie, bolts of lightning and great manifest power would jolt the victor with the reward of more power and author-ity. This movie scene has inspired me as a picture of the great power that is directed toward me, a Christian believer—the resurrection power that raised Jesus to the highest place in the heavens.

I have often prayed that God would just hit me with a bolt of lightning that would change my life, that the "lightning of God" would flow into my life from above.[3]

I have found over the years that the resurrection power of God flows through me when I slay the enemy one Scripture at a time, thereby killing the flesh of my ignorance and setting free the Spirit of God that lives in me, as I die to small and insignificant events. Although I seldom feel the power surge, I do see the fruit of His love and power through a yielded instrument (me) in signs and wonders and prophetic exhortation to others. On those days when I open a Scripture book forged between God and I, a very real "Highlander" experience happens and I understand afresh that there can be only "One." Oh what a joy it is to know the One who is Jesus Christ!

## PASSING OUT JEWELS

Your Scripture books will become a living prophetic experience in your life as you gather your treasure chest of jewels. But when God tells you to give away a truth or profound revelation, understand that it is yours to give. Remember that "the secret things belong to the Lord our God, but the things revealed belong to us and to our sons forever, that we may observe all the words of this law" (Deuteronomy 29:29).

Peter understood this truth when he said to the crippled man begging for alms at the Beautiful Gate that he (Peter) didn't have any money, "but what I do have I give to you: In the name of Jesus Christ the Nazarene—walk!" (Acts 3:6). This is the ministry of Jesus—"the words which You gave Me I have given to them..." (John 17:8).

The beauty is that the Word of God is truly the bread of life, and as you give it away, it will multiply in your life. It feeds you and others at the same time, yet still remains with you to give away again.

God moves in countless directions and ways. As you use your Scripture books, you will begin to see that the movement of the Father is in multiplication, not just addition. When you use the Word of God, it becomes a living demonstration of how God multiplies spiritual gifts and anointings that you are then able to impart to others on His behalf. He has "considered [you] faithful" and has entrusted you with His Word (1 Timothy 1:12).

## HOPEFUL INVITATION

I recall hearing Heidi Baker, when she was visiting our area, tell the story of how God took her in the Spirit into His presence and showed her different rooms in heaven. One room had tables with lots and lots of food on each of them. Then there was another room filled with body parts for the sick and dying— replacement parts that were more than enough.

Another room had a very small door, and she had to get on her face to enter through it . When she did enter in, the doorway opened to a chamber with the Father where she could just sit in His lap, love Him, and be loved by Him.

Her visions and experiences can be dismissed as imagination or used as a holy invitation for us to come into a deeper place in God. But be warned: this kind of intimacy with the Father will cost you more than you have been willing to pay up to this point. Heidi's experiences and visions are an invitation to live beyond our understanding and current experiential place in God. Once there, you will feel like you would have given more to have received such personal attention from Papa.

I counsel you to hear and believe the Father's hopeful invitation, to hear His voice say to you, "Come up here; let us dine together—just you and I—in the quiet place of your heart." Ride the wind of Jesus' prayer for you: "Father, I desire that they also, whom You have given Me, be with Me where I am, so that they may see My glory which You have given Me, for You loved Me before the foundation of the world" (John 17:24).

We must keep moving forward toward the living God, pressing into a new understanding and experience of Him. A body in motion stays in motion. Don't be satisfied with just knowing about Him. Touch Him and let Him touch your life and clothe you in His glory and love.

## NOTES

1.  I heard Bill Johnson say this in one of his sermons.

2.  *Highlander,* directed by Russell Mulcahy (1986; Beverly Hills, CA: Starz/Anchor Bay, 2002), DVD.

3.  John G. Lake, a great man of God, would often speak of these "lightnings of God."

## Chapter 7

# A COUNSELING TOOL

*I have more insight than all my teachers, for*
*Your testimonies are my meditation.*

—PSALM 119:99

*The Lord God has given Me the tongue of disciples,*
*that I may know how to sustain the weary one with*
*a word. He awakens Me morning by morning,*
*He awakens My ear to listen as a disciple.*

—ISAIAH 50:4

## INVALUABLE FOR COUNSEL

As a counseling tool, your Scripture book is invaluable for all the obvious reasons. Counselors know that emotional stroking may soothe a person's anxiety for the moment, but equipping that person to deal with the circumstances of their life is the goal.

Psalm 1 speaks about the wise man seeking counsel:

*How blessed is the man who does not walk in*
*the counsel of the wicked, nor stand in the path*

*of sinners, nor sit in the seat of scoffers! But his delight is in the law of the Lord, and in His law he meditates day and night. He will be like a tree firmly planted by streams of water, which yields its fruit in its season and its leaf does not wither; and in whatever he does, he prospers* (Psalm 1:1-3).

It is important to note that the person in this psalm is not gathering opinion, but rather seeking truth. It is our place as men and women of God to have the truth that sets the captives free to give to others who are seeking counsel from us.

Jeremiah 1:12 says that God is "watching over [His] word to perform it." We are also reminded in Psalm 103:20 that the angels are waiting to perform the Word of God: "Bless the Lord, you His angels, mighty in strength, who perform His word, obeying the voice of His word!" (Psalm 103:20).

## COUNSELING WITH THE WORD

Michael and I took over a church when we moved to our present city. In the process of moving I became very ill. The illness digressed into walking pneumonia. During a coughing session I broke two ribs that then floated around inside of me. Needless to say it was very painful.

On one of my first days in the office at our new church, the secretary told me that I might want to consider canceling the next appointment on my calendar.

When I asked why, she told me that the woman with whom I would be meeting had killed every home group she ever attended. She was so needy that she drained every person with whom she came in contact. The leaders had to quit the group because they couldn't handle her anymore.

I called her to my husband's office and shut the door behind me. She was a large woman, very tall and dressed like a man. She began to go into her whole story as we started talking. After about ten minutes, I stopped her, told her I could help her and that I wanted to see her completely well but we would take this one step at a time.

We would deal with the first issue she mentioned. I confronted the issue with the Word of God. As she began to get irritated and insist that I listen to the rest of her story, I politely said it was my help that was being sought and I would give it as the Holy Spirit was leading me. I told her that a drowning person is not going to tell the rescuer how to rescue them. She immediately began to manifest like a snake, and I knew, with no special discernment required, that what was going on was demonic in nature. She jumped up and threatened to kill me. She swept all the objects off the desk as I went and stood in front of the door to prevent her from leaving the office and said to her, "For the first time in your life there is someone strong enough to love you. I will not give you sugar pills of acceptance. I will let the Holy Spirit deliver you from the demon that binds you and I will instruct your life with the power of the Word of God. Do you want my help?"

You have to remember that at this point I am standing in front of the door with broken ribs. As I said this, she lunged at me to hit me. My hand went up and caught her fist and she fell to the floor screaming, "You are hurting me!"

I took authority over the demon and asked her, "Do want deliverance?" She just kept screaming about how horrible I was. And you know what? That is true; to a demon I am horrible. But getting the woman to talk to me was what I needed at that time. When I was able to get her to talk instead of the demon, she told me she was just fine and didn't need any deliverance.

I explained that the voices she was hearing were not from God and that I could help her. She insisted that she was fine and needed no help. I then instructed her that there is new leadership here and that she was not allowed to call people from our church or to go to our home groups until she completed her counseling session with me, which included deliverance. I loved her enough to not let her stay in that condition. Did she want my help? She said emphatically, "No!" I let her know that when she was ready for help, we would be here for her. I let her leave, and as soon as she was clear of the office, she ran screaming out of the building.

That may seem harsh to some readers, but it is actually far worse to do deliverance on someone who does not want it. This is because, as Jesus instructed us in

Matthew 12, the demonic force will return more powerfully without the power of the Holy Spirit occupying the empty places in the person that have just been vacated through deliverance. Jesus said:

> *Now when the unclean spirit goes out of a man, it passes through waterless places seeking rest, and does not find it. Then it says, "I will return to my house from which I came"; and when it comes, it finds it unoccupied, swept, and put in order. Then it goes and takes along with it seven other spirits more wicked than itself, and they go in and live there; and the last state of that man becomes worse than the first* (Matthew 12:43-45).

The Holy Spirit is going to come to those with a willing heart, not a resistant one. For we know that God resists the proud but gives grace to the humble (see James 4:6). Deliverance would have done more harm than good for this particular woman.

In our trips to South America and to other third world countries, it has been our experience that one of the strategies of the enemy is to get a person to receive deliverance without being filled with the Holy Spirit immediately afterwards. Whenever a person is not filled with the Holy Spirit after deliverance, the demonic powers can come back into the defenseless person more powerfully than they were before.

It is very important when we counsel people and lead them into freedom that they are filled with the

Spirit of God and equipped with the Word of God in order to resist the enemy when he seeks to return. Make no mistake about it: Jesus said that the enemy would seek to return (see Matt. 12:43-45).

## SPEAKING ONE COUNSEL

For this reason all of the leaders in our church speak one counsel, which is the voice of the Word of God on our lips. We have one voice. It is a core value that we hold high. As many of you know, many people like to go from person to person to hear what they want to hear about their particular problems or circumstances. If that happens in our church, you are going to get Scripture from everyone to whom you go. You may get different Scriptures, but you will mainly get the Word of God as counsel. Those who just want someone to agree with their position quickly get identified and will either grow, which is our goal, or eventually leave.

As the categories of your Scripture book increase and as you continue to meditate on the Word, allowing the Spirit to give you insight and understanding, you will be filled with "armor," which becomes your arsenal of treasures to give away. Your meditation on the Word will make you wise and give you living words to give away to the weary (see Isa. 50:4).

We know that there are times when we need to help others put on their own armor, times when we need to give them ammunition to fight the good fight of faith and see how they can let the battle and the victory be the Lord's. At other times we will need to give them the treasure of heaven and the bread of life, but as you do these things, always remember the power of the Word abiding within you. His Word is available for others, and yet it also remains in you, waiting to be given away. His abiding Word is the blessed bread of life, and it continues to multiply as we give it to hungry hearts.

I know that as you counsel others, you will experience the value of your Scripture book and all the hours you spent in prayer creating this book. When the storms come, you will be proclaiming from the rooftops the things you have heard as a whisper from Him, just as Jesus promised in Matthew 10:27. You will experience great joy as you witness what you have stored up inside of you through personal communion with God overflow as wisdom for those you counsel.

For those of you who are not gifted or called as counselors, your Scripture book is still invaluable as a tool to help others. We are all called to speak "the truth" to one another "in love," and to give grace to each other by speaking words of encouragement (see Eph. 4:15,29). When someone has turned to you for help, how much more can they be helped if we give them the Word of God rather than a concerned opinion? "You can all prophesy," as First Corinthians 14:31 says—which means we can all provide exhortation, edification, and comfort to others by speaking the Word of life to a friend in need (1 Corinthians 14:31).

If all believers would invest the time to forge the Word of God in their hearts, the lost and the seeker would find a safe place to learn and grow. Then the believers would be ready, as Peter instructed us:

> ...*always being ready to make a defense to everyone who asks you to give an account for the hope that is in you, yet with gentleness and reverence* (1 Peter 3:15).

I always know when someone is getting ready for leadership in our church because they place a high value on the Scripture, which is the Word of God. When I see someone beginning to create a Scripture book, when I see them bringing it to church and using it when they pray for others, then I know that the fruit of their life will change and grow in abundance and that character and heart are not far behind. When I see God grooming His leaders in this way, it is easy to bless what He is doing.

And we see once again the Scriptures fulfilled:

> *On that day the deaf will hear words of a book, and out of their gloom and darkness the eyes of the blind will see. The afflicted also will increase their gladness in the Lord, and the needy of mankind will rejoice in the Holy One of Israel* (Isaiah 29:18-19).

> *...I have written to you, young men, because you are strong, and the word of God abides in you, and you have overcome the evil one* (1 John 2:14).

The Word of God plays a very important role in speaking the truth in love and providing godly, biblical counsel to those around us. Not only is it useful in giving direction to those seeking counsel, but creating a Scripture book can have powerful effects on your teaching and preaching ministry as well.

*Chapter 8*

# A SERMON AND TEACHING TOOL

*And Jesus said to them, "Therefore every scribe who has become a disciple of the kingdom of heaven is like a head of a household, who brings out of his treasure things new and old."*
—MATTHEW 13:52

*All Scripture is inspired by God and profitable for teaching, for reproof, for correction, for training in righteousness; so that the man of God may be adequate, equipped for every good work.*
—2 TIMOTHY 3:16-17

## FRESH BREAD FOR TEACHING

Now that you have categorized the Word of God in your Scripture books into neat subjects, you will begin to see from book to book themes that appear over and over again. This is because the Scriptures used in your books are Scriptures with revelation for you. Revelatory

Scriptures increase your ability to release anointing on your teaching because you are not giving from intellectual knowledge but from revelatory experience.

Teachers who are truly gifted release anointing that opens the realm of the Kingdom of God for the miraculous. That is why every time an anointed man or woman of God teaches, there are signs and wonders that confirm the Word. First John 3:8 says, "The Son of God appeared for this purpose, to destroy the works of the devil" (1 John 3:8). Understanding is an experience. We must require an experience of what we believe. Without the power of God demonstrated by His Word, we are left only with religion.

Our good friend and associate Randy Clark frequently teaches on how "God can use little ol' me!" God used Randy as His instrument that opened the gate for the outpouring of the Holy Spirit in Toronto. In what became known as the "Toronto Blessing," thousands of people came from all over the world every day to get a touch of the fire of God. It has been two decades since God began to move through Randy in Toronto, and people continue to come and experience God's anointing and presence. In just a few weeks' time, John and Carol Arnott, pastors of the Airport Vineyard Church where it all began, went from being a small church to becoming a church that hosted people from all over the world. To this day a great move of God continues in that place.

Randy was pastoring a small church in Missouri when God called him to Toronto. He did not know why God would use him to open such a great gate of empowerment to bless the wider Body of Christ. All of that Kingdom expansion took place because as a simple act of obedience, Randy went to say what he heard God say, and God showed up very powerfully.

When I teach at conferences and churches, I always want the fresh bread of life to give away to those I'm teaching-not a "leftover" sermon or someone else's message downloaded from a website or found in someone's sermon book, but the fresh Word of God. I turn to my Scripture books for living bread. Forged over the years, these little books give me fresh revelation because they are the recipe books of my life and my experience with my heavenly Papa. As I pour through my Scripture books, I ask Him what I am to serve the people that particular day. "What meal do You want me to prepare for this group of people?" I ask.

## RENEWING YOUR MIND THROUGH LIVING IN HIS WORD

I recall teaching for four days at a women's retreat a few years ago. On the third day, I wore my dad's overalls to the conference. When I walked into the room, the women were giggling and having a good time. Soon after I began to speak, it became apparent why I was in my dad's britches. I was making a point that even if I did not fill them out the way he did, I had been given the right to wear them because they belonged to my father—I had inherited them. It was not my dad who was present but his covering on me. What I did in that covering was up to me: I could go farm, ride a horse, relax at the pool, or preach the Word of God.

Once you and the Father have created your new "Scripture britches"—your Scripture book—it is up to you as to how you use it. In many respects, the spirit is subject to the prophet, as the Scripture says (see 1 Cor. 14:32).

At this retreat I told the women that if there were only one sermon I could ever teach them, one thing in life I could give and impart that would last a life-time, the lesson I would teach would be the one about the renewing of our minds through living in His Word. For in the renewing of our minds we become the instrument of the Word of God and that which the hand of the living God can use for His purposes and His glory. With a renewed mind we become a vessel of honor in His house. The renewed mind is a tuned instrument. When the fingers of the Father play you and His breath flows through you, the proper sound and tone are released through your seasoned spirit and personality.

The renewed mind is a mind that knows the Lord-ship of the King of kings, and it possesses the strength and the resolve to know that the impossible is truly possible. I have found that my Scripture books have served as a wonderful tool in the loving hands of the Holy Spirit in the process of renewing my mind, and I know that it will be the same for you as well. Any sermon or teaching you ever give is going to be flavored with the anointing between you and your Father. And the required result is that those we teach have an experience from God by the life we release from our time with God.

## Chapter 9

# JOURNALING THE VISIONS, DREAMS, AND REVELATIONS

*Then the Lord answered me and said,*
*"Record the vision and inscribe it on tablets,*
*that the one who reads it may run."*
—HABAKKUK 2:2

### DAY-TO-DAY WHISPERS

I have found that it is important to keep a section in my Scripture book free so that I can write down the day-to-day whispers of the Father. I encourage you to do this as well, and be sure to date each of your entries. I have found over the years that it helps to see how many years ago God spoke a particular Scripture that continues to bring encouragement in the present. Whenever He directs me to revisit an entry, the date of that entry reveals when it was that God installed that particular truth in my life. In this way, I have a record of the "seeding time" and can trace the fruit of that seed in my life.

These day-to-day whispers are seed revelations that God uses to chart the course for future events and strategies for the advancement of His Kingdom in my life and ministry, and as I speak into the lives of others. They are the mapping of things to come in the journey. I am always excited when I pick up one of my Scripture books, written and dated years ago, and read the revelations that have actually been fleshed out in my life and teachings.

The same holds true for dreams that are empowered by the Holy Spirit. I urge you to record in your Scripture book any dreams that you sense are from God and date them so that you can look back and see the dross of life being removed and the gold of life being revealed.

## INTERPRETING OUR DREAMS

We often don't know the interpretation of a dream or vision at the moment we receive it. But after a bit more experience and study, clarity emerges.

I love how Kris Vallotton, Senior Leader of Bethel School of Supernatural and pastoral staff of Bethel Church in Redding, California, teaches that "God is not an American and His first language is not English." Kris thinks that God's first language is pictures, not words. Our heavenly Father speaks to us in many different ways, through pictures, images, phrases, thoughts, memories, dreams, and visions. His language is a love language that comes to us in different ways depending on what He knows we need in the moment. I have found that when I write down these God impressions, it helps me to discern His voice. All of your senses are communication ports.

If you are like me, there are many times when you have had a powerful dream or vision and you think that you will never forget it, but have found that time has a way of sifting powerful experiences and disempowering them. After a while, you can't remember the details of the dream or vision. You may even start adding to the experience until it gets diluted and is not what God was showing you in the first place. The cure for this ill is to write down your dreams and visions as soon as you receive them from the Lord. In this way, you can revisit them in the future, allowing God to direct you and give you fresh revelation and discernment. In the process He will give you markers to keep you on track as He leads you to your Kingdom destiny. Make sure to map these markers diligently.

If you don't immediately understand God's whispers, don't dismiss them. He is faithful to teach us His ways as we continue to follow Him. Just remember His promise from Isaiah:

> *I will lead the blind by ways they have not known, along unfamiliar paths I will guide them; I will turn the darkness into light before them and make the rough places smooth. These are the things I*

*will do; I will not forsake them* (Isaiah 42:16 NIV).

Remember Job 33 as you experience His dreams:

*Indeed God speaks once, or twice, yet no one notices it. In a dream, a vision of the night, when sound sleep falls on men, while they slumber in their beds, then He opens the ears of men, and seals their instruction* (Job 33:14-16).

There is one foundational principle about dream interpretation that may help you in your journaling. Most dreams from God communicate revelation about you, your heart, and your life. This is true the majority of the time, even when other people are present in the dream. Remember Joseph's dream in Genesis 37? Joseph dreamt about his brothers and parents bowing down to him (see Gen. 37:5-8). Do you remember King Nebuchadnezzar's dream in Daniel 4? As Daniel said to the King, "It is you, O King"—the tree in the king's dream was a parable of the king's own heart and life (Daniel 4:22).

There is so much more to say about dreams, but let me reiterate one point one more time: begin your inquiry into the meaning of a dream with the simple thought that the primary message of a "God dream" is usually about you, your heart, and your life. It is not necessarily about the other people in your dream. This simple, though profound understanding will assist you in opening up revelation as you meditate on what God is saying to you through your dreams.

## JOURNALING IN YOUR SCRIPTURE BOOK

This "free" section of your Scripture book can also be used for journaling other important things the Lord speaks to you about—those things that are directional and revelatory. This section can often be the most intimate part of your Scripture book. It is fuel for the fire that forges the ore of the Word you have excavated in order to create the living sword of God in your life and heart.

We must be good soldiers of Jesus Christ and fight the good fight of faith, holding tight to His eternal life (see 1 Tim. 6:12). I exhort you again that the more you sweat in training, the less you will bleed in the battle.

Take the time to love the journey you are on. Many of us don't enjoy the process until we get there, wherever there is. I urge you to enjoy the process of getting to where God is leading you. Remember, you are the one who determines the direction of your journey, and you are the one who decides to stop and enjoy the vista or blast on down the road. Tarry with God awhile and discover the hidden treasures of the dreams as His revelations tug on your heart. If you don't take time for the process, you will leave God's treasures undiscovered on the path of time.

# HOW DO I START MY SCRIPTURE BOOK?

### TAKE THE FIRST STEP

Let me encourage you to start your Scripture book immediately, today. Every journey begins with a resolve to travel, followed by the first step. If you're not able to begin today, I encourage you to start as soon as possible because the longer you put it off, the better the chance you won't start at all, depriving yourself of an amazing journey with God. Do not let lack of "proper" supplies keep you from the treasures of His voice to you. Use whatever you have on hand, be it a spiral notebook, a loose-leaf folder, or just loose paper.

Your first step does not have to be complicated. Keep it simple. Begin by asking yourself, "What Scripture is giving me life, encouraging me, or speaking something special to me right now?" When God whispers the answer, write it down. You have just begun the process of creating a Scripture book. If you can't think of a Scripture that is currently encouraging you, then start reading Psalms or any of the Gospels and listen for His voice in His Word. Jesus loves you, and you will receive from Him if you ask Him. He said, "My sheep hear My voice" (John 10:27). When you find a verse that resonates in your heart, write it down. In this way, the process will begin. Once your journey has commenced, you will never be the same, as the hand of the Father shapes you to be more and more like Jesus.

Often group settings help us to discipline ourselves to complete what is in our intention. Create a study group that works on Scripture books and come to each one sharing the fresh revelation that they have found. Breaking the bread of life, iron sharpens iron. This is an excellent way to find new Scriptures as you see the life in a word for another. This group dynamic often accelerates understanding as the synergy of the group. It becomes a threshing floor and a training ground for all to sweat and teach one another not to bleed in the heat of war and overcoming circumstances of life.

## MY PRAYER FOR YOU

I want to pray for you now as you hold this book:

*I pray an impartation of the Spirit of God to fill your life and passions. That you would hunger and thirst for all of Jesus and be filled with all the fullness of God. I release transformation of the Word of God to complete you and cause you to be all God designed you to be in His Kingdom.*

*I also ask that the gifting you now have and the gifting you will receive will multiply and become an inheritance for you, your children, and an inheritance you can give to others so that their portion may be full. May it multiply in you as the bread of heaven.*

*I bless you to become the living Word of God manifest as the Bride of Christ, equally yoked with her Groom, empowered by the Word and the Spirit of God, moving in perfect synchronization with Jesus. I bless you to be strong and bold as the Warrior Bride.*

*The time you spend in acquiring this wonderful weapon and intimate knowledge of God will empower your life and the lives of others. I pray that you will begin to have cognitive understanding of the invisible and witness the tangible Kingdom of God being released into time by you.*

*I give to you from the treasure of my life and from my spiritual inheritance, that your inheritance and that which you pass to your succeeding generations shall be enriched. I add to your portion. I spiritually impart to you by these pages what God has placed in me and upon me; that which I have fought for and have learned I freely give to you. I ask that your wealth may have a fuller measure, pressed down, shaken together, and running over. I bless you, my brothers and sisters in Christ Jesus. I remain His servant and yours. Amen.*

# HOW CAN I KNOW JESUS?

You may have read this book and be wondering, "How can I know Jesus like this woman seems to know Him?" I want to share with you briefly about how you can know Jesus Christ personally and forever.

First, let me remind you that we, as humans, have been created in God's image. That means we are a spirit and have a soul, which is the mind, will, and emotions, and we live in a physical body. In our culture, we are so accustomed to identifying and attributing everything we experience to the body and the soul. Yet if you have ever attended a funeral and looked at the person in the casket, you know that is not them; it is just the way you identified them. They are not there, not as a person. They have passed on. They were the laughter, and they were the passion. They were the hardworking, caring, loving person that inhabited that body. Yet, at the same time, we are more than our thoughts and emotions. What drives all the passion, joy, and love is our spirit. It is not until death that we actually experience the division of the three parts—the body, soul, and spirit.

Let's now consider how we come to know Jesus in an intimate and personal way. We come to know Him when we have a spirit-driven release of our heart and allow our emotions to be set aside along with mental assent. If you will allow yourself to be vulnerable by opening your spirit and trusting God to demonstrate to you the way you view the world and process thoughts, then you will be exercising what God calls faith. He knows you, and He knows how to demonstrate Himself to you. He knows how to touch your heart, your mind, and your emotions, and to allow you to begin to experience His presence in a personal way.

Experiencing God is more than goose bumps or a few tears; it is a true knowing in your heart, a knowing in which you comprehend that the God of the entire universe is full of love and attention for you. He is extravagant and intimate, and He knows *you*!

Remember how I told you God is not American and His first language is not English but that He speaks in pictures and imagery? That is why it is important to ask God to sanctify (set apart) our imagination for holiness. It is in this way that He shows us who He is. These events are often described as visions or dreams. God says in the Bible that He will speak to us in dreams and visions (see Job 33:15). Allow your heart to open up, and then invite Jesus to come into your heart and demonstrate the love God has for you. Invite Him to encounter you on the level of the body, soul, and spirit The Scriptures say no one comes to the Father except though Jesus (see John 14:6).

There is a price to pay to be in the presence of God, and that price is holiness. We, in our state of sin, cannot enter into His presence of our own accord. It would destroy us because we are so full of sin and death (see Rom. 3:23). Jesus came and gave us His glory and took our sin and death so that we can experience the presence of God (see 2 Cor. 5:21). He takes our death, and we inherit the relationship with the Father that was stolen so long ago in the Garden of Eden. We get His life.

No other teacher, prophet, or person of any nature has ever or can ever give us access to the Holy God of all creation except Jesus. Invite Jesus to make the spirit exchange with you. Ask the Holy Spirit to come and fill you with the presence of God, and then wait and listen.

It is very important to listen at this point. It is not necessary to keep your eyes closed, but if things easily distract you, you may want to close your eyes and focus on God, allowing Him to begin to show you His love.[1] You will often experience your emotions being filled to the fullest capacity with joy and peace. As this comes, anger, stress, and frustration will fade away in God's presence, until you can come into the fullness of experience. It is important to ask for forgiveness for your self-centered lifestyle and the sins you know you have committed.

It is important to note at this point to forgive others that have sinned against you as God has forgiven you. If you hold on to the sins of others who have harmed you, it will be difficult to come into the fullness of God. No sin can be in His presence. Let go of the sins others have done to you; Jesus paid for all sin and every evil that has been done to you. Those who have hurt you are sinners just like you and me, and we're not perfect. You have hurt and destroyed people with your words and attitudes too. There is power in forgiveness. It would be good at some point to ask those you have hurt to forgive you so they are not held in your sin.

Your mind may battle with you at this point; the soul is very powerful, for it was created that way for a purpose. Uncharted territory for the soul is always a battle. That is why the Scriptures say we must renew our minds (see Rom. 12:2). We must allow the transformation of spiritual reality to be the leader of our thoughts rather than the desires of our body, which has been catered to our entire life. The body doesn't like being told not to be in charge. The whole process of writing a Scripture book will help in this transformation.

Now that you know the "why," here is the "how." Let's pray:

> *Father, in the name of Jesus I come to You and ask for forgiveness for my sins and the sins I have committed toward others. I forgive those who have sinned against me, for I am in need of forgiveness. I ask that You would encounter my heart, my soul,*

*and my spirit today. I want to know that You're really there and love me. Let Your forgiveness flood over me and wash away my fear, my pain, and my anger, my shame, all of which are displeasing in Your sight.*

*I believe in Your Son, Jesus, that He came and paid the price for my sin so that I could have the privilege of coming to You now. I believe He was resurrected from the dead and stands at Your right hand interceding for me. I believe that the Holy Spirit will be sent to me to fill me with power and the knowledge of Your presence.*

*Come into my life; I surrender to Your will and ask that You daily show me a better way of peace, joy, and love in this life. I ask that You would open my understanding and let me know Your voice. Here I am, Lord Jesus, come into my life.*

*Give me revelation of Your Word. Let it be alive to me as I read and study the Scriptures; let me see You in the Scriptures. Quicken them to my life and mind that I might hunger and thirst after Your presence. Amen.*

The Word of God encourages us to be filled with the Holy Spirit and power (see Acts 1:8; Eph. 5:18). In the book of Acts, we see the Holy Spirit coming on the people with power, signs, and wonders. It is the same power of the Holy Spirit that comes to you when you get saved. It is the transformation for which we just prayed. But there is a baptism of the Holy Spirit that is an overflowing of the power and presence of God that I believe is vital for any Christian to experience in order to live a life in the supernatural realm. When this baptism happens, it comes with gifts and evidence of God's Spirit.

One of those signs is "speaking with other tongues." There is a fullness that fills your soul and spirit to such a degree that it must be expressed, and the words you know seem futile and incomplete. So God gives the language of "tongues" to express this passion and love and the evidence of His Spirit in you. It may be the tongue of another known language or the language of angels. Either way, this gift, even though it is considered the least of the gifts, is very powerful. And it comes with supernatural wonders of its own.

The Scriptures remind us to have the elders of the church come and lay hands on us, that we may receive the Holy Spirit. This is so that the elders, who are experienced in the Holy Spirit, can discern along with you what is happening in the spiritual. The actual release and power does not come from the hands of the elders, but it comes from the Holy Spirit Himself. It is the Father who does the work (see John 14:10). I myself received the Holy Spirit when I was alone, reading prayers. Many others have also received the Holy Spirit when no one else was present.

Likewise, the actual laying on of hands in the physical is not what matters most. What matters most is what is being released in the realm of the Spirit. Right now I lay hands on you in the spirit through the pages of this book and ask for the Holy Spirit to come in power over your mind, will, and emotions. I ask for the Holy Spirit to come in power over your body, soul, and spirit right now. I pray:

> *Holy Spirit I invite Your presence. Lord Jesus, come and overshadow your children, right now, as they read this prayer. May the baptism of the Spirit of God come on them right here, right now. Be filled with, be baptized in, and overflowing with the presence of God and His Spirit in the Name of Jesus. I ask this with the evidence of Your Spirit, which gives gifts and transforms our lives. Your Word says you will fill us with the Spirit and Power and Fire.*

As the presence of God increases on you, allow your spirit to be filled and then speak to God face to face in the voice and language He has just given to you. Don't limit yourself to your known languages. Allow the intimacy of the Holy Spirit to create a new language that is filled with His presence. It may sound like a foreign dignitary speaking; it may sound like a love language; it may start with just a few syllables; but the more you use your tongues, the more easily they will flow. There are nine gifts of the Spirit and nine fruits of the Spirit.[2] You will begin to see the evidence of all these take place in your walk with God as you are filled with His presence.

We are to walk in the fullness of the glory of God. That is what Jesus paid for, not just fire insurance. From glory to glory He changes us, but it is up to us to work out our own salvation on a daily basis (see 2 Cor. 3:18; Phil. 2:12). When we stumble, we only have to ask for forgiveness once again and receive His cleansing. We now have the Holy Spirit in us. We choose when we pray in the Spirit and when we open our mouth and speak in tongues—the Scripture says the spirit is subject to the prophet so it is subject to our will (see 1 Cor. 14:32). When we are hungry and passionate after the Lord and His presence, we talk to Him several times a day. We press into the high calling of the holiness of His presence. And we live life to the fullest and capture the journey of revelation in Christ and all He has done and is doing in these last days.

If these are the last days before the return of Christ, then so be it. However, I am not deceived. They are my last days before I walk into glory with Him so I live them accordingly. Be not weary in well-doing, having done all to stand, and continue to stand (see Gal. 6:9). Knock, and the door will be opened to you; seek, and you shall find (see Matt. 7:7).

So again I pray:

> *Holy Spirit, I invite Your presence. Lord Jesus,*
> *come and overshadow your children, right now,*
> *as they read this prayer. May the baptism of the*
> *Spirit of God come on them right here, right now.*
> *Be filled with, be baptized in, and overflowing*

*with the presence of God and His Spirit in the Name of Jesus. I ask this with the evidence of Your Spirit, which gives gifts and transforms our lives. Your Word says you will fill us with the Spirit and Power and Fire.*

## NOTES

1. When we pray with our eyes open, we do so in order to see what God is doing.

# About the Author

For more information or other teaching resources from Mike and Cherrie you can contact them at:

Kingdom Legacy
2774 Cobb Parkway NW suite 109 #316
Kennesaw, Ga. 30152
or email at
contact@KingdomLegacy.org

# RESOURCES

## "STUDY GUIDE FOR CLAIMING YOUR INHERITANCE"

This valuable tool aids the reader or study group to easily begin or to continue the process of becoming the living Word and step into the authority of the Word and intimacy with the heavenly Father. Practical application through questions and assignments allows a rich ground for the seed of life to take root, encouraging the reader or study group to own and experience transformation and truth, and not just take in information.

## "ADVENTURE OF SUPERNATURAL DISCOVERY"

The adventure begins the moment you realize that there has got to be more. If you find yourself hungering for more of a face-to-face encounter with God, you owe it to yourself to read this book. If you are in a dry place and are longing to be refreshed again, God is ready. This book will awaken the reality of a heavenly Father who wants to engage His family with tangible experiences. It will unlock a depth of intimacy and revelation that will change your life forever. You will come to a place where the "more" of God has become a reality, and you will never be the same.

## "RELEASING HEAVEN THROUGH INTERCESSION"

This is a two-part CD set in which Cherrie Kaylor explains levels of intercession and then prays with you concerning healing. The entire second CD is praying healing Scriptures. If you are in need of healing or have someone that needs healing, then you may want to consider this set. The testimonies that have come back have been amazing.

## "HEALING THE BROKEN PAST"

This set will bring you into a place of wholeness and freedom and will help erase the effects of your past. Sometimes the patterns repeat and we feel like we are going around the mountain again. God has an amazing destiny for you. Letting go of the past will free you to move forward into your divine destiny.

To view other resources or to order visit:
www.KingdomLegacy.org

# THE ADVENTURE *of* *a* LIFE-TIME

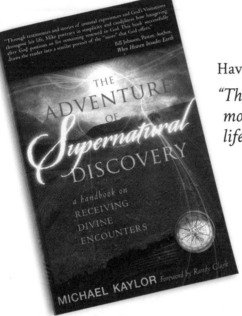

Have you ever thought,

*"There has got to be more to the Christian life than this"?*

Well, there *is!*

**Normal Christianity has been redefined over the centuries.** What began as a vibrant encounter with the Living Christ through the power of the Holy Spirit has often become formulaic and stale. If this is you, then it's time for you to get a new normal.

Author Michael Kaylor shares his personal testimony of redefining normal and stepping out on the supernatural adventure that transformed His relationship with God forever.

### In this book, discover God's vision for normal Christianity...

*Prophetic dreams and visions • Impartations • Uncontainable joy*
*Divine appointments • Supernatural healing and miracles*

**Take the journey and discover the supernatural life
God has destined you to live!**